Ukrainian Banking Regulation

# International Banking and Securities Law



Volumes published in this Brill Research Perspectives title are listed at *brill.com/rpbs*

# Ukrainian Banking Regulation

*Its Challenges and Transition towards European Standards*

*By*

Olga Afanasyeva
Armin J. Kammel

BRILL

LEIDEN | BOSTON

Originally published as Volume 2(1) 2017, in International Banking and Securities Law, DOI 10.1163/24056936-12340005.

The Library of Congress Cataloging-in-Publication Data is available online at http://catalog.loc.gov
LC record available at http://lccn.loc.gov/2018945605

Typeface for the Latin, Greek, and Cyrillic scripts: "Brill". See and download: brill.com/brill-typeface.

ISBN 978-90-04-38141-4 (paperback)
ISBN 978-90-04-38142-1 (e-book)

# Contents

# Contributors

*Olga Afanasyeva, Ph.D.*
Executive Director, Ukrainian Venture Capital and Private Equity Association (UVCA)

*Anton Boiko, Ph.D.*
Associate Professor, Department of Economic Cybernetics, Education and Research Institute for Business Technologies Sumy State University

*Evgeniia Chukhareva, M.A.*
Graduate Research Assistant, Lauder Business School (LBS), Vienna, Austria

*Dr. Armin J. Kammel, LL.M., MBA*
Prof. (FH) of Banking Law and Securities Regulation, Lauder Business School (LBS), Vienna, Austria

*Serhiy Lyeonov*
Professor, Department of Finance, Banking and Insurance, Sumy State University

*Tetiana Vasylieva*
Professor; Director of Academic and Research Institute of Finance, Economics and Management, Sumy State University

# Introduction

This monograph is devoted to analyzing and assessing the transformation of banking regulation and supervision in Ukraine against the background of the EU-Ukraine Association Treaty of 2014. Since the gradual move of the Ukrainian banking environment towards EU standards is full of challenges, the monograph explains not only the principles, functions, tasks and specifics of the existing system of banking regulation but also to assess the implications of the reform process of the bank regulatory environment in Ukraine.

The dominance of government regulation and the rarely existing niches of self-regulation are structural features of Ukrainian banking regulation that have to be taken into consideration during the ongoing reform process because they also reflect the "culture" of banking regulation in Ukraine which may differ from many other jurisdictions in this respect. Along these lines, the developments of the Ukrainian banking system not only differ somewhat from Western standards but also show some distinct features compared to some other post-Soviet countries. Consequently, the ongoing transformation of the Ukrainian regulatory environment towards EU standards has some specific aspects, which particularly will be pointed out.

In order to gain a better understanding of these aspects, one has to reflect on both the geographical location of Ukraine and its originally insignificant coverage of banking services for the population. One also has to account for the rapid and partially uncontrolled inflow of – in particular – European capital into the Ukrainian banking sector of Ukraine from 2005 until the Global Financial Crisis (GFC). A prime example of this period was the acquisition of Bank "Aval" by the Austrian Raiffeisen Bank International.

This transaction demonstrated the far-reaching effects of the application of European requirements on Ukrainian bank organizations, especially regarding the internal management of banking processes. However, this modernization period of the Ukrainian banking industry almost came to a standstill due to the GFC, leading to significant capital outflows beginning in 2009. Although the momentum of modernization due to European ownership of Ukrainian banks is now gone, the relative share of foreign capital in the Ukrainian banking system roughly remained the same due to increased investments from the Russian Federation. Thus, recent Russian investments have also contributed to the reshaping of the banking system in Ukraine.

Another aspect of consideration is the current fragile environment in Ukraine, which is closely linked to the military conflict in the Eastern part of the country and the annexation of Crimea by Russia. The pending tensions between Ukraine and Russia in this context have triggered the imposition of harsh conditions on Russian capital in the Ukrainian banking sector with the policy objective to strengthen the role of Ukrainian state banks.

When addressing particularities of the Ukrainian banking system, it is also important to refer to the dependence of the Ukraine on the National Bank of Ukraine due to the current political situation in the country. Thus, this dependence has significant practical implications on the treatment of certain systemically important financial institutions owned by oligarchs. These individuals, who are supportive of certain political interests, may try to influence the National Bank for the sake of their business operations.

Against this background, the current Ukrainian efforts to adapt its system of banking regulation and financial supervision to EU standards is causing a significant transformation of the domestic banking system. Thus, this monograph intends to provide a thorough understanding of the mechanisms of the Ukrainian banking system, its stages of development, its transition towards EU standards and its future prospects towards a strengthened European integration process.

# Ukrainian Banking Regulation: Its Challenges and Transition towards European Standards

*Olga Afanasyeva, PhD*
Ukrainian Venture Capital and Private Equity Association (UVCA)
*o.b.afanasieva@gmail.com*

*Armin J. Kammel*
Lauder Business School; California Lutheran University
*akammel@callutheran.edu*

## Abstract

For the last years, Ukraine and particulalry its financial sector were seeking to gradually apply and comply with EU standards. Latest with the signing of the EU-Ukraine Association Agreement in 2014 the transition towards EU standards has a formal basis. Since then, Ukraine – with strong support from the EU – is in the process of implementing legislative and regulatory measures in order to comply with this Agreement. Against this background, this contribution wants to shed some light into Ukraine's efforts as well as to explain some of the complexities of this process by providing an in-depth background of the current Ukrainian banking regulation, its economics and the challenges of complying with new EU standards.

## Keywords

Ukraine – banking regulation – EU-Ukraine Association Agreement – banking system – EU financial regulation – implementation of EU standards

## 1 The Transition of Ukrainian Banking Regulation

The recent period of Ukrainian history, starting from its declaration of independence and culminating in the signing of the EU-Ukraine Association

 | DOI:10.1163/9789004381421_002

Agreement[1] in 2014 (which entered into force on 1 September 2017), has been characterized by an increased emphasis on the efficient management of Ukrainian banks. This was triggered by external factors such as the multiplicity of the economic crises and the increased integration of global finance.

In order to better understand the transition of banking regulation and supervision in Ukraine, as well as the rationales and reasons of recently introduced reforms, it is important to reflect on the history of the formation of Ukrainian banking. This reflection should focus on the principles of Ukrainian banking as well as the efforts to implement European principles of banking regulation.

From its independence in 1991, an independent Ukrainian banking system emerged. The system is regulated by domestic banking legislation such as the law "On banks and banking activity"[2] which had been adopted by *Verkhovna Rada*[3] in March 1991. Following that law, the Ukrainian Branch of *Gosbank*[4] which used to be the State Bank of the USSR, was transformed into the currently existing and independent National Bank of Ukraine (NBU).[5]

After its establishment, NBU started with the registration process for Ukrainian banks. This registration process is based on the above described new legal framework for banks which generally lays out the basic principles of Ukrainian banking law. Consequently, the law "On banks and banking activity" can be considered as the first attempt to regulate and supervise banking business in Ukraine. Nevertheless, it is also worth stressing that the law "On banks and banking activity" did not include many issues related to market entry aspects of banks such as:

- deadline for reviewing registration documents was not defined;
- procedure for obtaining licenses for each type of banking activity was unclear;

---

1 EU-Ukraine Association Agreement: http://trade.ec.europa.eu/doclib/docs/2016/november/tradoc_155103.pdf.

2 On banks and banking activity: Law of Ukraine from 20.03.91 # 872-XII – Access mode: http://zakon3.rada.gov.ua/laws/show/2121-14.

3 On the procedure for the creation, registration of commercial banks: Temporary provision of the NBU from 17.07.92 # 16. – Access mode: http://zakon2.rada.gov.ua/laws/show/v0016500-92.

4 Leshchenko V. V. (2013) Organizational and legal mechanism of functioning of banking control in Ukraine. Pages 274–282. – Access mode: http://nbuv.gov.ua/UJRN/Nvamu_upravl_2013_3_36.

5 Economic standards for the regulation of commercial banks: Resolution of the NBU from 21.12.93 # 114, – Access mode: http://zakon5.rada.gov.ua/laws/show/v0114500-93.

- procedure for the opening the branches and representative offices was not defined for foreign banks.[6]

These concerns were answered in the temporary resolution "On the Order of Establishment, Registration of Commercial Banks".[7] It defined the business relationships of commercial banks in Ukraine. Moreover, the establishment of the Department of Banking Supervision by the NBU played an important role in the further development of the Ukrainian banking system. It also led to necessary amendments of the regulatory and supervisory framework for commercial banks in the country.[8]

Another step in the development of legal framework for commercial banks in Ukraine has been Regulation "On Economic Standards of Regulation of Commercial Bank's Activity"[9] issued in 1993. This regulation served as the basis for prudential banking supervision. It introduced regulatory measures such as authorized minimum capital requirements, liquidity balance indicators; solvency requirements for banks; required minimum reserves to be placed on a special account with NBU; and maximum risk exposures.[10]

However, these developments faced drawbacks in relation to the implemented regulations. One of these drawbacks was the simplified licensing procedures which caused incidents due to the establishment of numerous unstable banks across Ukraine in the period 1991–1993. In order to eliminate regulatory loopholes, the NBU and the Government of Ukraine had to adopt new regulations in order to strengthen the bank regulatory framework.

One legislative response was the approval of the decree "On Currency Regulation and Currency Control"[11] in February 1993 which introduced basic principles for foreign exchange market activities. Moreover, this decree

6 On the System of Currency Regulation and Currency Control: Decree of the Cabinet of The Ministers of Ukraine from 25.11.1993 # 3651-XII. – Access mode: http://zakon3.rada.gov.ua/laws/show/15-93.

7 Dyakonova I. (2008) Methodological foundation for the modernization of the banking supervision in Ukraine on the basis of leading indicators. – Sumy, Ukrainian Academy Of Banking.

8 Approval of the Regulation of economic standards for the actions of commercial banks: Resolution of the NBU from 21.12.1993 # 114. – Access mode: http://zakon2.rada.gov.ua/laws/show/v0114500-93.

9 Credit activities: Resolution of the NBU from 28.09.1995 # 246 – Access mode: http://zakon2.rada.gov.ua/laws/show/v0246500-95.

10 On the Procedure of Cash Operations in the National Economy of Ukraine: Resolution of the Board of the National Bank of Ukraine from 02.02.1995 # 228. – Access mode: http://zakon3.rada.gov.ua/laws/show/v0228500-95.

11 Aborchy O. V. (2013) Analysis of the evolution and the current state of the banking system of Ukraine. Strategy and mechanisms of regulation of industrial development. – P. 193–209. – Access mode: http://nbuv.gov.ua/UJRN/sim_2013_2013_17.

introduced the cashless turnover of Ukrainian Karbovanets,[12] which were later, in September 1996, replaced by the new currency, called Hryvnia (UAH).[13]

In this context, it is worth mentioning that the introduction of the national payment system[14] in January 1994 hugely contributed to the empowerment of cashless payments, the information collection on payment transactions and the reduction of cases of using counterfeit paper payment documents. In July 1994, the Resolution of the National Bank of Ukraine was approved. It defined the status, functions, rights, duties and tasks of the authority of NBU. Moreover, it led to a convergence of supervisory bodies as well as initiated of banking supervisory activities carried out by the regional offices of NBU.[15]

NBU's Banking Supervision Department was created in 1995 and constitutes the basis of Ukraine's banking supervisory infrastructure (Figure 1). Additionally, banking operations licensing was approved during the same year.[16]

In the same year, triggered by the implementation of Resolution "On urgent measures for financial rehabilitation of commercial banks and restoring of their liquidity"[17] NBU's Regulation # 114 on economic standards was repealed. As a replacement, a new NBU resolution "On economic standards of commercial banks"[18] was accepted, which introduced mandatory liquidity requirements, solvency standards, minimum amounts of authorized capital and risk exposures on a client level.[19]

12 On the procedure of regulation and analysis of the activities of commercial banks: Resolution of the NBU from 14.04.98 # 141 – Access mode: http://zakon3.rada.gov.ua/laws/show/z0323-98.

13 Methodological guidelines for the inspection of commercial banks and banking institutions in Ukraine: Resolution of the NBU from 30.12.96 # 344 – Access mode: http://zakon.nau.ua.

14 On the Procedure for the Establishment and Registration of Commercial Banks and On the Procedure for Licensing Banks in Ukraine: Resolution of the NBU from 27.03.96 # 77. – Access mode: http://zakon3.rada.gov.ua/laws/show/v0077500-96.

15 On the Commission of the National Bank of Ukraine on Supervision and Regulation of Banks: Resolution of the NBU from 09.11.98 # 470. – Access mode: http://zakon2.rada.gov.ua/laws/show/v0470500-98.

16 The structure of the system of banking supervision of the National Bank of Ukraine and its authority to adequately respond to violations in the activities of commercial banks: Resolution of the NBU from 17.11.97 # 380. – Access mode: http://zakon2.rada.gov.ua/laws/show/v0486500-97.

17 Lepinsky I. (2008) Essence and main characteristics of banking regulation: herald NBU. – # 10. – C.66–67.

18 Rajewski K. E. (2003) Banking Supervision: Educational-methodical manual for self-learning. – Kyiv. – 174 p.

19 On the application by the National Bank of Ukraine of measures of influence on commercial banks for violation of banking legislation: Resolution of the NBU from 04.02.98 # 38. – Access mode: http://zakon3.rada.gov.ua/laws/show/z0177-98.

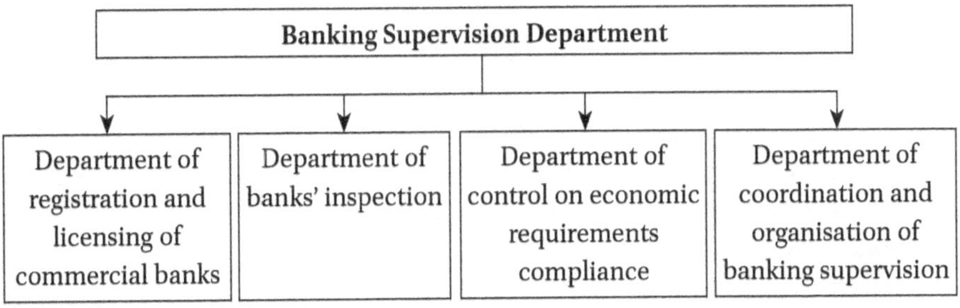


FIGURE 1 Structure of Banking Supervision Department in Ukraine in 1995[20]

Furthermore, the adoption of the Regulation of the NBU "On crediting"[21] of September 1995, led to the establishment of the main principles regarding the provision of loans, its usage and repayments, as well as relationships of the parties of loan business. In addition to this, NBU recommendations "Order of cash transactions in the economy of Ukraine"[22] served as a basis for cash payments realization. In 1996, NBU both established the Commission on Supervision and Regulation of Bank Activities[23] and issued a corresponding Resolution "About National Bank of Ukraine",[24] which defined its objectives, rights and regulations.

A further advancement of the system of banking regulation in Ukraine was achieved with adoption of NBU's instruction "On order of regulation and analysis of activity of commercial banks",[25] that introduced twenty-one standards and additional indicators on bank performance. However, this instruction had been replaced by the corresponding instruction "On Financial Services and State Regulation of Financial Services Markets"[26] in 1998, which also incorporated international standards of accounting and reporting.

---

20 Rajewski K. E. Banking Supervision: Educational-methodical manual for self. Learn Dists/. – K. : КНЕУ, 2003. – 174 p.

21 On the Procedure for Granting Banking Licenses for Banking Operations: Resolution of the NBU from 06.05.98 # 181 – Access mode: http://zakon3.rada.gov.ua/laws/show/z0373-98.

22 On Approval of the Instruction on the Procedure for Regulating and Analyzing the Activities of Commercial Banks: Resolution of the NBU from 14.04.1998 # 141 – Access mode: http://zakon2.rada.gov.ua/laws/show/z0323-98.

23 Official website of the Deposit Guarantee Fund. – Access mode: http://www.fg.gov.ua/.

24 On National Bank of Ukraine: Law of Ukraine from 20.05.1999 # 679-XIV. – Access mode: http://zakon4.rada.gov.ua/laws/show/679-14.

25 On banks and banking activity: Law of Ukraine from 20.03.91 # 872-XII. – Access mode: http://zakon3.rada.gov.ua/laws/show/2121-14.

26 On Financial Services and State Regulation of Financial Services Markets: Law of Ukraine from 12.07.2001 # 2664-III. – Access mode: https://www.microfinancegateway.org/sites/default/files/mfg-en-paper-law-on-financial-services-and-state-regulation-of-financial-services-markets-2005.pdf.

The incorporation of international standards in domestic Ukrainian banking legislation was also already introduced in 1996 with the introduction of the NBU "Guidelines for the inspection of commercial banks and banking institutions in Ukraine",[27] Regulation of the Verkhovna Rada of Ukraine (VRU) "On the procedure of establishment and registration of the commercial banks"[28] and Resolution of the NBU "On the licensing of banks in Ukraine".[29] The aim of these was to better assess the specific risks of banking business.

In addition, Regulation of the NBU "On the Commission on the supervision and regulation of banks"[30] grants the Commission specific powers regarding the licensing of banking institution. In line with these developments, the updated Regulation of the NBU "On the Commission of the National Bank of Ukraine on supervision and regulation of banking activity"[31] granted this new authority a broader range of competencies to be able to respond to market changes in a timelier manner.

Given the multiplicity of individual legislative acts, the consolidation of Ukrainian legislation on banking supervision took place in the adoption of the Regulation of the NBU "On the structure of the system of banking supervision of the National Bank of Ukraine and its authority to adequately respond to violations in the activities of commercial banks".[32]

Another development concentrated on the introduction of a concise methodology for banking supervision. This led to the establishment of the Advisory Council on Banking Supervision and Regulation[33] in 1997. This institutional change also reflects the expanded duties of NBU's Banking Supervision Department, which – as Figure 2 displays – consists of 4 sub-departments and one independent body.

NBU has also been pushing for the transition of the Ukrainian banking system towards the application of international accounting standards. This would

27 The procedure of planning and of conducting inspections: Resolution of the NBU from 17.07.2001 # 276. – Access mode: http://zakon2.rada.gov.ua/laws/show/z0703-01.

28 On The Deposit Guarantee Fund for Individuals Deposits: Law of Ukraine from 20.09.2001 # 2740-III. – Access mode: http://zakon3.rada.gov.ua/laws/show/2740-14.

29 On the Procedure for Regulating the Activities of Banks in Ukraine: Resolution of the NBU from 28.08.2001 # 368. – Access mode: http://zakon3.rada.gov.ua/laws/show/z0841-01.

30 On the application by the National Bank of Ukraine of the measures of influence for violation of banking laws: Resolution of the NBU from 28.08.2001 # 369. – Access mode: http://zakon2.rada.gov.ua/laws/show/z0845-01.

31 The procedure for rating ratings on the CAMELS rating system: Resolution of the NBU from 08.05.2002 # 171– Access mode: http://zakon2.rada.gov.ua/laws/show/v0171500-02.

32 Kostenko V. V. Retrospective of the formation and development of banking supervision in Ukraine. Economics and state. – 2014. – # 10. – C. 80–84.

33 On the procedure for compiling and publishing financial statements of banks of Ukraine: Resolution of the NBU from 07.12.2004 # 598. – Access mode: http://zakon2.rada.gov.ua/laws/show/z1660-04.

enable, for example, the reporting on a consolidated basis of affiliated banking groups. The respective legal basis was the adoption of Regulation of the NBU "On the application by the National Bank of Ukraine the measures of influence on commercial banks for banking laws violation".[34]

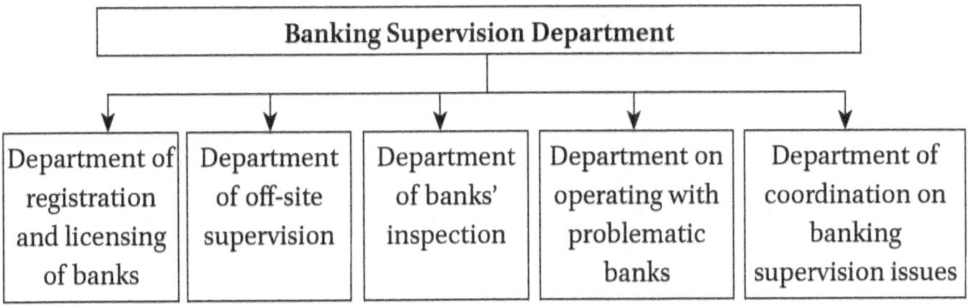


FIGURE 2 Structure of Banking Supervision in Ukraine in 1997[35]

In addition, the mechanism of banking licensing was improved which led to changes in the overall system of banking supervision and regulation.[36] In this light, it is worth noting that the adoption of Regulation of the NBU "On the mechanism of licensing of banks for banking operations conduction"[37] was an accompanying feature.

Additionally, Regulation of the NBU "Instruction on the regulation and analysis of commercial banks activity"[38] played an important role. The reason for it is that it specified the procedure of early response and preventive measures, the application of penalties in case of breaching performance indicators as well as expanded the range of economic analysis of banking activities. Also in 1998, the Deposit Guarantee Fund[39] for depositors of commercial banks in

34 Methodological instructions for the inspection of banks "Risk Assessment System": NBU Guidelines from 15.03.2004 # 104 598. – Access mode: http://zakono.rada.gov.ua/laws/show/v0104500-04.

35 Rajewski K. E. Banking Supervision: Educational-methodical manual for self. Learn Dists/. – К. : КНЕУ, 2003. – 174 p.

36 On Approval of Methodological Recommendations on the Organization and Functioning of Risk Management Systems in Banks of Ukraine: Resolution of the NBU from 02.08.2004 # 361 – Access mode: http://zakon4.rada.gov.ua/laws/show/v0361500-04.

37 On Approval of the Methodology for Calculation of Economic Norms for Regulating the Activities of Banks in Ukraine: Resolution of the NBU from 02.06.2009 # 315 – Access mode: http://zakono.rada.gov.ua/laws/show/v0315500-09.

38 On Amending some Legislative Acts of Ukraine Regarding the Peculiarities Recovery of Banking: Law of Ukraine from 24.07.2009 # 1617-VI – Access mode: http://zakon2.rada.gov.ua/laws/show/1617-17.

39 Procedure for the formation of reserves by banks for loans and accrued interest and write-off of bad debts: Resolution of the NBU from 13.09.2010 # 424 –Access mode: http://zakon2.rada.gov.ua/laws/show/z0998-10.

Ukraine, was set up by the passing of the Decree of the President of Ukraine "On Measures to Protect the Rights of Physical Persons as Depositors of Commercial Banks in Ukraine".[40] This led to a significant increase in consumer confidence in the Ukrainian banking system.[41]

A new development stage of the Ukrainian banking supervisory system had been reached with the adoption of the Law of the VRU "On the National Bank of Ukraine".[42] It included a separate section on "Banking regulation and banking supervision", which defined the functions of NBU, its purpose and scope in this respect. The structural reform in sub-departments of banking supervision was also introduced in this context, which established an organizational structure comprising of the Department of Prudential Supervision, the Department of Methodology and Coordination of Banking Supervision and Cooperation with Financial Institutions and the Department of Supervision on the International Activities of Banks.

According to the Law of the VRU "On banks and banking activity"[43] which had been adopted in 2000, the Ukrainian system of banking regulation and supervision had been further improved by reflecting a further convergence of domestic banking legislation to European standards. In this regard, the main directions of reforming domestic banking supervision had been defined by implementing its new structure in accordance with the principles for effective banking supervision set out by the Basel Committee.[44] Basel principles describe the rules of effective bank supervision, licensing and structure of the institution, regulation of activities, application of banking supervision methods, requirements for information, powers of banking supervisors, conditions for international banking. These rules reflected in the creation of the General Department of Banking Supervision (Figure 3).

---

40 On approval of the procedure for granting banks and branches of foreign banks general licenses for currency transactions: Act of NBU from 08.09.2011 # 306 – Access mode: http://zakono.rada.gov.ua/laws/show/z1203-11.

41 On approval of the Regulation on the Procedure for Organizing and Conducting Inspections on Prevention and Counteraction to the Legalization (Laundering) of the Proceeds from Crime or the Financing of Terrorism: Resolution of the NBU from 20.06.2011 # 197 – Access mode: http://zakon5.rada.gov.ua/laws/show/z0852-11.

42 On Households Deposit Guarantee System: Law of Ukraine from 23.02.2012 # 4452-VI – Access mode http://zakon4.rada.gov.ua/laws/show/4452-17.

43 On measures aimed at promoting banks capitalization and restructuring: Law of Ukraine from 28.12.2014 # 78-VIII – Access mode http://zakono.rada.gov.ua/laws/show/78-19.

44 Basel Committee – Core Principles Access mode: http://www.bis.org/list/bcbs/tid_25/index.htm.

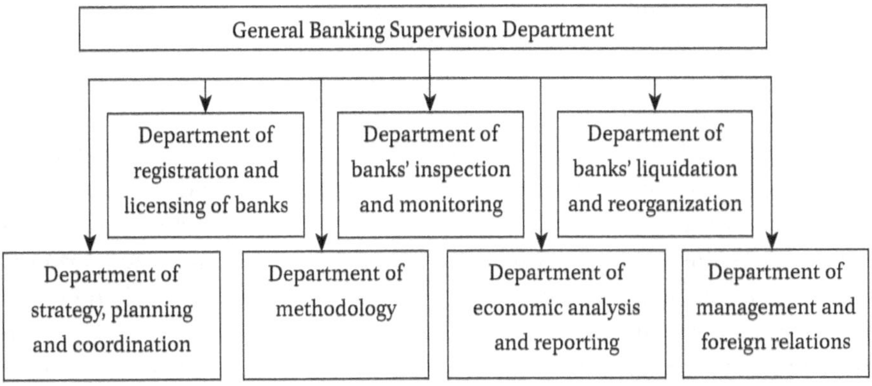


FIGURE 3 The structure of the General Banking Supervision Department in Ukraine in 2000[45]

In 2001 the Law of the VRU "On financial services and state regulation of financial markets"[46] had been adopted, which assumed that banking organizations are financial institutions, and their exclusive activity is to provide financial services. This law also lays out general principles regarding to the regulation of financial services as well as the implementation of regulatory and supervisory functions conducted by the respective authorities. Through the adoption of Regulation of the NBU "On the procedure of issuing to banks of banking licenses, written permits and licenses to perform certain operations"[47] in 2001, the licensing process had been improved and Regulation of the NBU "On the planning and conducting of inspections in banks" further improved the supervisory process.[48]

Moreover, the Law of Ukraine "On Deposit Guarantee Fund (DGF)", which had been adopted in 2001, set out the relationship between the DGF and NBU with the purpose to better protect depositors. With the adoption of Instruction of the NBU "On the order of regulation of banks' activity in Ukraine"[49] thirteen

45 Rajewski K. E. Banking Supervision: Educational-methodical manual for self. Learn Dists/. – К. : КНЕУ, 2003. – 174 p.

46 On financial services and state regulation of financial markets: Law of Ukraine from 12.07.2001 # 2664-III – Access mode: http://zakon3.rada.gov.ua/laws/show/2664-14.

47 On the procedure of issuing to banks of banking licenses, written permits and licenses to perform certain operations: Resolution of the NBU from 17.07.2001 # 275 – Access mode: http://zakon2.rada.gov.ua/laws/show/z0730-01.

48 On the planning and conducting of inspections: Resolution of the NBU from 17.07.2001 # 276 – Access mode: http://zakon2.rada.gov.ua/laws/show/z0703-01.

49 On the order of regulation of banks' activity in Ukraine: Resolution of the NBU from 28.08.2001 # 368 – Access mode: http://zakon2.rada.gov.ua/laws/show/z0841-01.

mandatory standards of commercial banks have been introduced, which allowed to analyze and cover the main aspects of the various banking activities.

The system of measures influencing banks was improved by the adoption of Regulation of the NBU "On the application by the National Bank of Ukraine of the measures of influence for violation of banking laws".[50] Furthermore, Regulation of the NBU "On the procedure for determination of ratings on rating system CAMELS"[51] allowed NBU to carry out specific supervisory actions regarding banking activities based on risk assessment criteria. Also, certain changes have been made in the structure of NBU bodies that are engaged in supervision and regulation. The two new departments set up were the Department of Inspection and the Department of Off-site Banking Supervision. The functions of the previous 7 departments in the structure of the General Banking Supervision Department were integrated in to four established 4 departments (Figure 4).

With the rationale to facilitate an effective banking supervisory structure in Ukraine, NBU classified all banks into four groups according to their respective total assets: the largest, large, medium and small banks. The supervisory powers in relation to the first two groups were delegated to the General Banking Supervision Department.[52] The other two groups are under the supervision of both General Banking Supervision Department and NBU's regional branches.

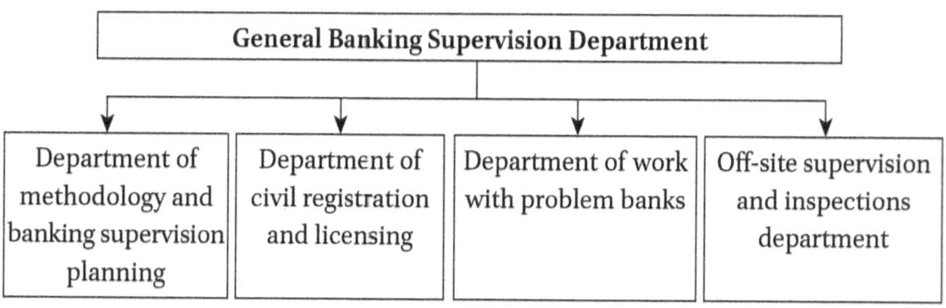


FIGURE 4 The structure of the General Banking Supervision Department in Ukraine in 2003[53]

50 On the application by the National Bank of Ukraine of the measures of influence for violation of banking laws: Resolution of the NBU from 28.08.2001 # 369 – Access mode: http://zakon5.rada.gov.ua/laws/show/z0845-01.

51 On the procedure for determination of ratings on rating system CAMELS: Resolution of the NBU from 08.05.2002 # 171 – Access mode: http://zakon2.rada.gov.ua/laws/show/v0171500-02.

52 Kostenko V. V. Retrospective of the formation and development of banking supervision in Ukraine. Economics and state. – 2014. – # 10. – C. 80–84.

53 Konopatska L.V. Banking Supervision: academic textbook – KNEU, 2008. – 336 p.

By reflecting on the consolidation trend in the Ukrainian banking sector, NBU approved the Regulation of the NBU "Instructions on the procedure for the preparation and publication of financial statements of banks in Ukraine".[54] According to these instructions, the parent bank is obligated to submit consolidated accounting statements to NBU. Additionally, NBU issued guidelines for the inspection of banks labeled Resolution of the NBU "The System of Risk Assessment".[55] The guidelines determine the methods of risk assessment in banks subject to the NBU Regulation "Guidelines on the organization and functioning of risk management system in banks in Ukraine".[56]

In 2005 the structure of banking supervision was reformed once more. New supervisory authorities[57] were established. The supervisory structure was comprised of the Department of Banking Regulation and Supervision, the Department of Methodology for Banking Regulation and Supervision, the Department of Registration and Licensing, the Department of Preventing of the Usage of the Banking System for Money Laundering and Terrorism Financing. In 2006, these departments have been subordinated to the newly established Directorate of Banking Regulation and Supervision (Figure 5).

The following laws constitute the legal framework in the sphere of prevention and counteraction to the legalization (laundering) of the proceeds from crime or financing terrorism:

- Law of Ukraine "On Prevention of and Counteraction to the Legalization (Laundering) of the Proceeds from Crime, or Financing Terrorism";[58]
- Law of Ukraine "On banks and banking activity";[59]

---

54 Instructions on the procedure for the preparation and publication of financial statements of banks in Ukraine: Resolution of the NBU from 07.12.2004 # 598 – Access mode: http://zakon3.rada.gov.ua/laws/show/z1660-04.

55 Methodological instructions for the inspection of banks "Risk Assessment System" (Методичні вказівки з інспектування банків "Система оцінки ризиків"): NBU Guidelines from 15.03.2004 # 104 598. – Access mode: http://zakono.rada.gov.ua/laws/show/v0104500-04.

56 Guidelines on the organization and functioning of risk management system in banks in Ukraine: Resolution of the NBU from 02.08.2004 # 361 – Access mode: http://zakon2.rada.gov.ua/laws/show/v0361500-04.

57 Leshchenko V. V. (2013) Organizational and legal mechanism of functioning of banking control in Ukraine. Pages 274–282 – Access mode: http://nbuv.gov.ua/UJRN/Nvamu_upravl_2013_3_36.

58 On Prevention of and Counteraction to the Legalization (Laundering) of the Proceeds from Crime, or Financing Terrorism: Law of Ukraine from 28.11.2002 # 249-IV – Access mode: http://zakon2.rada.gov.ua/laws/show/ru/249-15.

59 On banks and banking activity: Law of Ukraine from 07.12.2000 # 2121-III – Access mode: http://zakon3.rada.gov.ua/laws/show/2121-14.

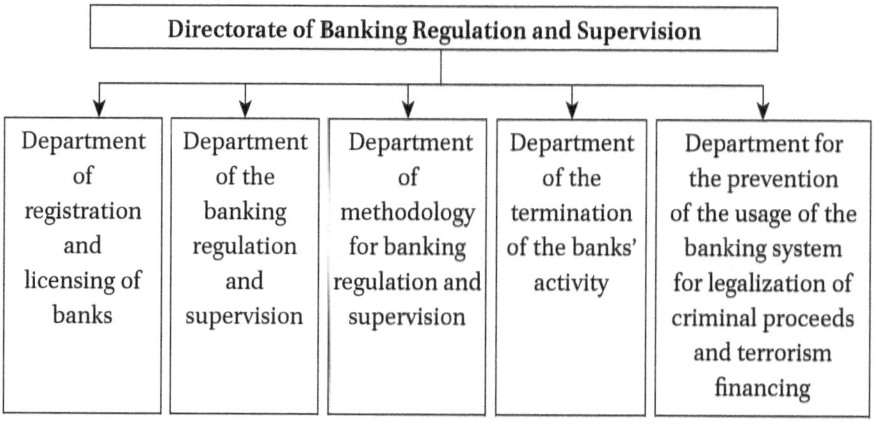


FIGURE 5 Structure of Directorate of Banking Regulation and Supervision in Ukraine in 2006[60]

- Criminal Code of Ukraine;[61]
- Code of Ukraine on Administrative Offenses.[62]

In 2008, the structure of banking supervision has been amended again, in particular from an institutional perspective since the Department of Banking Regulation and Supervision had been divided into the Department of Inspection and the Department of Off-site Banking Supervision.[63] Meanwhile, the departments of regional banking supervision had been reassigned to the regional branches of NBU's Directorate for Banking Regulation and Supervision (Figure 6).

In 2009, the standard-setting process in Ukrainian banking supervision had been improved by the adoption of guidelines of the NBU "The method for calculating economic standards of regulation of banks in Ukraine".[64] The guidelines primarily concentrate on recovery measures of banks which themselves had been subject to the Law of the VRU "On Amendments to Certain Laws Regarding Peculiarities for Financial Recovery Measures for Banks".[65]

60 Konopatska L.V. Banking Supervision: academic textbook – KNEU, 2008. – 336 p.
61 Criminal Code of Ukraine: Resolution of the VRU from 05.04.2001 # 2341-III – Access mode: http://zakon3.rada.gov.ua/laws/show/2341-14.
62 Code of Ukraine on Administrative Offences from 07.12.1984 # 8073-X – Access mode: http://zakon3.rada.gov.ua/laws/show/80731-10.
63 Konopatska L. V. (2008) Banking Supervision: textbook – KNEU. – 336 p.
64 The method for calculating economic standards of regulation of banks in Ukraine: Resolution of the NBU from 02.06.2009 # 315 – Access mode: http://zakon2.rada.gov.ua/laws/show/v0315500-09.
65 On Amendments to Certain Laws Regarding Peculiarities for Financial Recovery Measures for Banks: Law of Ukraine from 24.07.2009 # 1617-VI – Access mode: http://zakon3.rada.gov.ua/laws/show/ru/1617-17.

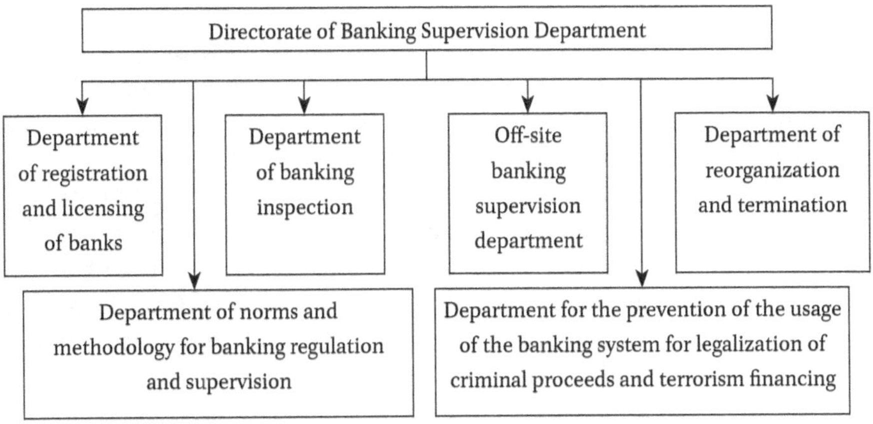


FIGURE 6 Structure of Directorate of Banking Regulation and Supervision in Ukraine in 2008[66]

In 2010, the new structure of the Banking Supervision Service at NBU had been implemented, establishing the Department of Crisis Management and Control of Market Operations. The duties and tasks were set out to deal with the pressing needs in banking supervision. Moreover, in order to facilitate the introduction of necessary liquidity levels in the Ukrainian banking landscape, Resolution of the NBU "Procedure of formation of reserves on loans and accrued interests on them and bad debts writing-off for banks"[67] was enacted.

In response to the Global Financial Crisis (GFC), the procedures for establishing banks had been significantly changed in 2011 in Ukraine. This was primarily done by the adoption of Regulation of the NBU "On the procedure of registration and licensing of banks, opening the separate departments".[68] The intention was to reduce the number of violations in the banking sector in the sphere of misappropriation of monetary funds. The decree Resolution of the NBU "On approval of the procedure for organizing and conducting inspections on prevention and counteraction to legalization (laundering) of proceeds from crime or terrorist financing"[69] was introduced in the same year.

66 Konopatska L.V. Banking Supervision: academic textbook – KNEU, 2008. – 336 p.

67 Procedure of formation of reserves on loans and accrued interests on them and bad debts writing-off for banks: Resolution of the NBU from 13.09.2010 # 424 – Access mode: http://zakon2.rada.gov.ua/laws/show/z0998-10.

68 On the procedure of registration and licensing of banks, opening the separate departments: Resolution of the NBU from 08.09.2011 # 306 – Access mode: http://zakon2.rada.gov.ua/laws/show/z1203-11.

69 On measures aimed at enhancing capitalization and restructuring of banks: Resolution of the NBU from 20.06.2011 # 197 – Access mode: http://zakon5.rada.gov.ua/laws/show/z0852-11.

In 2012, the duties of the Deposit Guarantee Fund had been expanded pursuant to the Law of the NBU "On the Guaranteeing of Deposits of Individuals".[70] The DGF had not only a regulatory, but also supervisory role, alongside NBU over the various business activities of commercial banks in Ukraine. The Fund's responsibilities also included the liquidation of insolvent banks.

In 2014, due to the political tension with Russia and the Russian invasion of Crimea, the Ukrainian banking industry experienced challenges. In an effort to, protect its economic security, rights, freedoms and legal interests of its citizens, Ukraine introduced measures to ensure the sustainability of its banking sector by strengthening its financial capacity. This was intended to minimize the negative impacts of the difficult economic environment of the country. This was reflected in the Law of the VRU "On measures aimed at enhancing capitalization and restructuring of banks".[71]

The Ukrainian system of banking regulation and supervision went through several significant challenges since the independence of the country in 1991. The multiple amendments to the various legal acts by NBU reflect the respective responses to the various challenges and threats to the financial system in the Ukraine. It is not surprising that most of these measures were related to issues of liquidity, capital requirements and risk management.

It has also become obvious, that the legislative framework of banking regulation and supervision in Ukraine is still in transition. The EU-Ukraine Association Treaty, which will be elaborated in more details later in this booklet, will have a significant impact on the regulatory framework for banks in Ukraine. Certain other regulatory procedures (for instance risk assessment) will need an additional formalization. Others (such as the specification of investment operations of banks) will need supplementary regulations.

## 2 The Economics of Banking Regulation in Ukraine

In the context of research being conducted regarding current mechanisms of banking regulation and supervision in Ukraine, it should be noted that according to Art. 1 of the Law of Ukraine "On the National Bank of Ukraine" # 679-XIV

70 On the Guaranteeing of Deposits of Individuals: Resolution of the NBU from 23.02.2012 # 4452-VI – Access mode: http://zakon4.rada.gov.ua/laws/show/4452-17.

71 On measures aimed at enhancing capitalization and restructuring of banks: Resolution of the VRU from 28.12.2014 # 78-VIII – Access mode: http://zakono.rada.gov.ua/laws/show/78-19-VI.

dated 20.05.1999, banking regulation is one of the responsibilities of the National Bank of Ukraine. The regulations establish the system, which regulates bank activities, determines the general principles of banking, procedures of banking supervision, and the responsibility for violation of banking laws.[72] According to Ukrainian legislation, banking regulation assumes only the establishment of a regulatory framework. Traditionally, however, the central bank's functions in countries typically works on a much larger scope. Similarly, the NBU is also not limited to legislative action. However, the restrictions of the law on the interpretation of "banking regulation" is indisputable.

Following the establishment of the statutory and regulatory provisions mentioned above, the NBU set out to create a framework for banking supervision. This framework sets out the system of controls and effective provisions to ensure compliance by banks and financial institutions. The NBU is taking supervisory actions to ensure the stability of the banking system of Ukraine as well as to protect the interest of depositors and creditors.

The interaction of the NBU with banks should be considered as both regulatory and supervisory. It consists of the establishment and adoption of a legislative framework of the mechanism of banks' supervision for compliance with established standards, and the usage of measures for stabilizing the banking system.

The main regulating legislation of banking activities in Ukraine are, as listed in Appendix 1, the following:

- Law of Ukraine "On the National Bank of Ukraine" # 679-XIV on May 20, 1999[73]
- Law of Ukraine "On banks and banking activity" # 2121-III dated 7 December 2000[74]
- NBU Regulation "On the procedure of registration and licensing of banks, opening the separate departments" # 306 dated 08.09.2011[75]

---

72 On the National Bank of Ukraine: Law of Ukraine from 20.05.1999 # 679-XIV – Access mode: http://zakon2.rada.gov.ua/laws/show/679-14.

73 On the National Bank of Ukraine: Law of Ukraine from 20.05.1999 # 679-XIV – Access mode: http://zakon2.rada.gov.ua/laws/show/679-14.

74 On banks and banking activities: Law of Ukraine from 07.12.2000 # 2121-III – Access mode: http://zakono.rada.gov.ua/laws/show/2121-14/paran1095#n1095.

75 On the procedure of registration and licensing of banks, opening the separate departments: NBU Regulation from 08.09.2011 # 306 – Access mode: http://zakon3.rada.gov.ua/laws/show/z1203-11.

- NBU Resolution “Resolution on the method for calculating economic standards of regulation of banks in Ukraine” # 315 dated 02.06.2009[76]
- NBU Resolution “On approval of Instruction of regulation of Bank Activities in Ukraine” # 368 dated August 28, 2001[77]
- NBU Board Resolution “On approval of the procedure of deposit transactions of Ukrainian banks with corporations and individuals” # 516 dated December 3, 2003[78]
- NBU Board provisions “On the planning and order of conducting inspections” # 276 dated July 17, 2001[79]
- NBU Board Resolution “On the application of the National bank of Ukraine standard instruments regulating banking system liquidity” # 615 dated 17.09.2015[80]
- NBU Board Resolution “On approval of the definition of banks in Ukraine credit risk from active banking operations” # 351 dated 30.06.2016[81]
- NBU Board Resolution “On approval of the foundations of the interest rate policy of the National bank of Ukraine” # 277 dated August 21, 2016[82]
- NBU Board Resolution “On the application of the National bank of Ukraine measures” # 346 dated August 17, 2012[83]

The main tasks of the National Bank of Ukraine, which has the mandate to supervise and oversee the management of the banking systems, are:

---

76 The method for calculating economic standards of regulation of banks in Ukraine: Resolution of the NBU from 02.06.2009 # 315 – Access mode: http://zakon4.rada.gov.ua/laws/show/v0315500-09/page.

77 On approval of Instruction of regulation of Bank Activities in Ukraine: Resolution of the NBU from 28.08.2001 # 368 – Access mode: http://zakon5.rada.gov.ua/laws/show/z0841-01/page5.

78 On approval of the procedure of deposit transactions of Ukrainian banks with corporations and individuals: Resolution of the NBU from 3.02.2003 # 516 – Access mode: http://zakon5.rada.gov.ua/laws/show/z1256-03.

79 On the planning and order of conducting inspections: Resolution of the NBU from 17.07.2001 # 276 – Access mode: http://zakon3.rada.gov.ua/laws/show/z0703-01.

80 On the application of the National bank of Ukraine standard instruments regulating banking system liquidity: Resolution of the NBU from 17.09.2015 # 615 – Access mode: http://zakon5.rada.gov.ua/laws/show/v0615500-15.

81 On approval of the definition of banks in Ukraine credit risk from active banking operations: Resolution of the NBU from 30.06.2016 # 351 – Access mode: http://zakon3.rada.gov.ua/laws/show/v0351500-16/page.

82 On approval of the foundations of the interest rate policy of the National bank of Ukraine: Resolution of the NBU from 21.04.2016 # 277 – Access mode: http://zakon3.rada.gov.ua/laws/show/v0277500-16.

83 On the application of the National bank of Ukraine measures of impact: Resolution of the NBU from 17.08.2012 # 346 – Access mode: http://zakon3.rada.gov.ua/laws/show/z1590-12.

- ensuring security and financial stability of the banking system;
- protecting the interests of depositors and creditors;
- creating a competitive and transparent banking sector;
- maintaining a high level of professionalism and standards in the banking sector.[84]

The system of banking regulation and supervision in Ukraine is based on a vertical framework and functions as a single mechanism with a central office – the National Bank of Ukraine. It has equal and inherent function for each of them with the right to make decisions and actions within the limits of given rights (Figure 7).

The National Bank implements the functions of banking regulations and supervision on an individual and consolidated basis. According to the Law of Ukraine "On banks and banking activity" # 2121-III from 07.12.2000, government regulation of banks is implemented in the form of administrative and indicative regulation.

The administrative regulations provides the following actions:

1. Bank registration and licensing of their activities
2. Establishment of requirements and restrictions for banks
3. Administrative or financial sanctions
4. Banking supervision
5. Recommendations on the activities of banks[85]

These forms operate in a systemic manner and constitute a complete management cycle through the NBU. However, it is worth mentioning that the fundamental and the first step for the implementation of this cycle is the fulfillment of legislative functions by the NBU. In this respect, NBU will promulgate regulations on the banking system. The regulations will be binding on of public authorities, local governments, banks, businesses and individuals.

The actions (instructions, regulations, rules) are adopted and approved in the form of NBU Board Resolutions. These resolutions do not contradict to the laws and other legislative acts of Ukraine, and are not retroactive, except in cases where they mitigate or cancel the responsibility according to the law. These actions of the NBU must be registered with the Ministry of Justice of Ukraine.[86]

84 On the National Bank of Ukraine: Law of Ukraine from 20.05.1999 # 679-XIV – Access mode: http://zakon4.rada.gov.ua/laws/show/679-14.

85 On banks and banking activity: Law of Ukraine from 07.12.2000 # 2121-III – Access mode: http://zakon3.rada.gov.ua/laws/show/2121-14.

86 Kovalenko V. V. (2013) Banking regulation and supervision: methodology and practice: monograph. – 491 p.

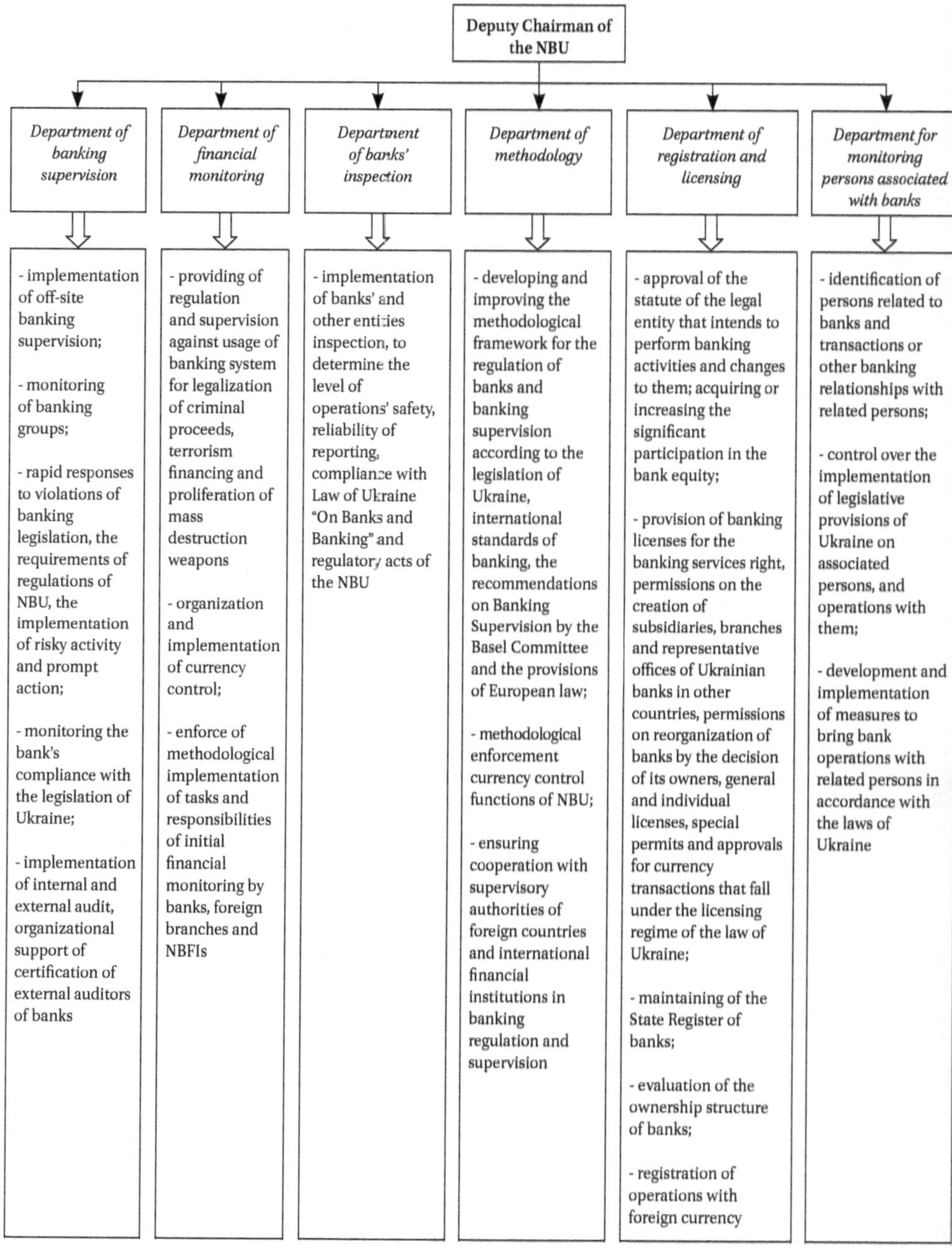


FIGURE 7 Structure of NBU departments in the sphere of banking regulation and supervision[87]

87 Made by the author.

The second stage is the access of institutions to the banking system, i.e. banks registration and licensing of banking activities. The purpose of the NBU is to regulate the possibilities of newly established banks or banks that plan to expand their list of ongoing banking operations and to operate according to the legislation of Ukraine and regulations of the NBU. By following NBU regulations, rules and procedures, institutions may conduct banking activities and obtain legal status. This process is governed by the order of bank registration and licensing conditions established by the Resolution of the NBU # 306 "On the procedure for banks registration and licensing, opening of stand-alone offices" dated 08.09.2011.[88] The basic requirement for entities to carry out banking activities is compliance with the NBU requirements and compliance with the current minimum authorized capital of state registration equaling at least 500 million hryvnias.

The state registration of entities is implemented by recording them in the Unified State Register pursuant to Ukrainian legislation. The eligibility criteria to receive a banking license requires that an institution submit all required documents to the NBU within a year prior to the date of state registration.[89]

The third step is banking supervision. The supervisory activities of the NBU cover the lower level of the banking system, i.e. all banks and their divisions, affiliates and related entities of banks in Ukraine and abroad, offices of foreign banks in Ukraine, and other businesses and individuals. Also, the NBU can use the services of other agencies under separate agreements for banking supervision. While supervising the institutions that provide banking activities in other countries, the NBU cooperates with the relevant authorities of those countries.

According to the Law of Ukraine, "On banks and banking activity", administrative supervision can be difficult and controversial pursuant to Law "On the National Bank of Ukraine", where these concepts require different forms of cooperation between NBU and other banks. Implementation of banking supervision is regulated by the laws of Ukraine "On the National Bank of Ukraine", "On banks and banking activity" and the Regulation "On the planning and conducting of inspections" # 276 approved by the National Bank of Ukraine on 17.07.2001 and others. First and foremost, the supervisory activity is focused on monitoring banks' compliance with established standards.

In conducting banking supervision, the NBU provides recommendations for ongoing activities. In case of deviations from the statutory or regulatory rules

88 On the procedure for banks registration and licensing, opening of stand-alone offices: Resolution of the NBU from 08.09.2011 # 306 – Access mode: http://zakon2.rada.gov.ua/laws/show/z1203-11.

89 On approval of the procedure for granting banks and branches of foreign banks general licenses for currency transactions: Act of NBU from 08.09.2011 # 306 – Access mode: http://zakono.rada.gov.ua/laws/show/z1203-11.

of the NBU, administrative or financial sanctions can be applied, depending on the nature and possible consequences of violations.

Pursuant to Art. 73 of the Law of Ukraine "On banks and banking activity" # 2121-III dated 07.12.2000, in case of violations by banks or other institutions, which are subject to inspection by the National Bank of Ukraine, or the conduct of risky operations that threaten the interests of depositors or other creditors of the bank, the NBU has the right to apply sanctions, appropriate to committed violation, which include:[90]

1) written warning to cease violations and implement appropriate measures to correct the situation, reduce unnecessary expenses of the bank, limit unnecessarily high interest payments on borrowed funds, or reduce or terminate inefficient investments;
2) organize a General Meeting of Supervisory Board members, the Board (Board of Directors) of the bank for adoption of a program of financial rehabilitation or restructuring plan;
3) enter into a written agreement, according to which the bank or an individual specified in the agreement is obligated to take measures to eliminate violations, or to improve financial condition of the bank.;
4) issue orders:
    a) suspending dividend payments or capital allocation in any other form;
    b) establishing increased economic standards for the bank;
    c) increasing reserves to cover possible losses on loans and other assets;
    d) restricting, suspending or terminating certain types of ongoing high-risk banking operations;
    e) prohibiting the making of unsecured loans;
    f) imposing fines on:
        - the managers of banks in an amount equal to one hundred untaxed minimal incomes of citizens;
        - banks, under the terms approved by the Board of the NBU, in an amount not greater than one percent from the registered authorized capital amount;
    g) temporary ban of the owner of a substantial participation of the bank's equity with respect to the voting rights of acquired shares in the case of a rough or systematic violation of the provisions of the

90 On banks and banking activity: Law of Ukraine from 07.12.2000 # 2121-III – Access mode: http://zakon3.rada.gov.ua/laws/show/2121-14.

Law of Ukraine "On banks and banking activity" or regulations of NBU, until the violation is remedied;

h) temporary removal of bank officials from their position, in case of rough or systematic violations by that individual of the requirements of the Law of Ukraine "On banks and banking activity" or regulations of NBU;

i) restructuring of the bank;

j) appointment of temporary administration.

In the case of a violation of this Law or regulations of NBU, which could lead to significant loss of assets or income, or the onset of insolvency of the bank, the NBU has the right to revoke the license and initiate the liquidation of the bank.[91]

The main stages of administrative regulations measured by the NBU are the following:

- regulation of access to the banking system. This provides the possibility to determine certain mandatory requirements and conditions to obtain a license; and second, establishing additional set of rules; and, third, supervision of compliance of these requirements and conditions;
- regular bank reports and inspections;
- enhanced supervision for problematic banks, including the prohibition of dividend payments, imposition of fines, application of sanctions etc.;
- implementation of special controls over insolvent banks, including the temporary administration of these banks, suspension of activities, reorganization and liquidation.[92]

According to the national legislation, another form is indicative regulation, which provide the National Bank with the following powers:

1) establishment of mandatory economic standards;
2) determination of mandatory reserves' standards for banks;
3) establishment of standards on allocations to reserves for covering the risks on active banking operations;
4) determination of interest rate policy;
5) recapitalization of banks;

---

91 The procedure of planning and of conducting inspections: Resolution of the NBU from 17.07.2001 # 276 – Access mode: http://zakon2.rada.gov.ua/laws/show/z0703-01. Moreover, see Shevchenko A. Financially-Legal Bases of Bank Regulation and Supervision in Ukraine: State and regions (Law). – 2014. V. 3. – 45–49 p. – Access mode: http://nbuv.gov.ua/UJRN/drp_2014_3_11.

92 Kovalenko M. M. (2011) Government regulation of the banking sector: the essence and components of the mechanism Theory and practice of public administration. – Access mode: http://nbuv.gov.ua/UJRN/Tpdu_2011_2_31.

6) regulation of correspondent banking relationships;
7) management of foreign exchange reserves, including currency intervention;
8) operations with securities at the open market,
9) controls over the import and export of capital.[93]

NBU has worked out "The method for calculating economic standards of regulation of banks in Ukraine" # 315 from 02.06.2009.[94] It sets economic standards for bank regulation, a procedure for the determination of regulation, including taking into account normative values. Standards are divided according to the areas of banking activities they regulate: capital, liquidity and credit risk.

Capital ratios require compliance with three indicators: the minimum regulatory capital (H1), the regulatory capital adequacy (H2), adequacy of fixed capital (H3).

The minimum size of regulatory capital (H1) of a bank, which obtained a banking license after 11 July 2014, should be USD 500 million before 11 July 2024. If the institution has received a banking license before 11 July 2014 (previous standard was UAH 120 million), the following phased gradation of bank capital replenishment is required:[95]

- UAH 120 million – before 17 June 2016,
- UAH 200 million – from 11 July 2017;
- UAH 300 million – from 11 July 2018,
- UAH 400 million – from 11 July 2019,
- UAH 450 million – from 11 July 2020,
- UAH 500 million – from 11 July 2024.

The regulatory capital adequacy ratio reflects the bank's ability to timely and fully pay its liabilities from trade, credit and other monetary obligations. The higher the capital adequacy ratio, the greater risk assumed by the bank owners. And vice versa, following the same logic, the lower the capital adequacy ratio, the greater risk assumed by the creditors/depositors. The bank is prohibited to pay dividends or allocate capital in any form, if such payment or allocation would violate this ratio.

H2 ratio is established for preventing an excessive shifting of bank credit risk and risk of default of bank assets to creditors/depositors. It is defined

93 On banks and banking activity: Law of Ukraine from 07.12.2000 # 2121-III – Access mode: http://zakon3.rada.gov.ua/laws/show/2121-14.

94 The method for calculating economic standards of regulation of banks in Ukraine: Resolution of the NBU from 02.06.2009 # 315 – Access mode: http://zakon4.rada.gov.ua/laws/show/v0315500-09/page.

95 On increase of capital of Ukrainian banks: Resolution of the NBU from 04.02.2016 # 58 – Access mode: http://zakon2.rada.gov.ua/laws/show/v0058500-16.

as the ratio of regulatory capital to total assets and certain off-balance sheet instruments, weighted by degree of credit risk after its reduction in the amount of:

- appropriate reserves from active banking operations;
- cash coverage;
- unencumbered government bonds refinanced by NBU, and debt securities issued by NBU, acquired under repo transactions (but not more than the amount under a separate transaction, which is included in the calculation of this ratio) with transferring of ownership on such securities.

During the calculation of regulatory capital adequacy to total assets and individual off-balance instruments weighted by the level of credit risk, the total amount of an open currency position of the bank in all foreign currencies and precious metals is added, and the value of uncovered credit risk is excluded. In order to calculate this indicator, the bank's assets should be divided into groups according to risk and then summarized for the appropriate weighting coefficients. H2 ratio value of operating banks shall not be less than 10 percent.

For banks, which are just initiating banking activity, this ratio should be:

- at least 15 % during the first 12 months of activity (after obtaining the license);
- at least 12 % over the next 12 months;
- at least 10 % in the future;

The ratio of capital adequacy (H3) is defined as the ratio of capital to total assets and off-balance liabilities, weighted on appropriate coefficients of credit risk. Standard value of H3 should not be less than 7 %.

The bank is required to create capital buffers (so-called capital conservation buffers), and countercyclical buffers which exceed the normative value of capital adequacy (H3).

The capital conservation buffer is calculated from the total amount of risk and should be equal to:

- since January 01, 2020 – 0.625%
- since January 01, 2021 – 1.25%;
- since January 01, 2022 – 1.875%
- since January 01, 2023 – 2.5%.

The countercyclical capital buffer is calculated from the total risk in the amount of 0–2.5%. In case of significant credit activity of banks and considering risks associated with excessive credit growth, its size is set by the Board of NBU. The information above is placed in advance at the official website of the National Bank and contains the information about the buffer size, and the buffer implementation date.

The liquidity ratio assumes compliance by banks to the following indicators: instant liquidity ratio (H4), current liquidity ratio (H5), short-term liquidity ratio (H6).

Instant liquidity ratio (H4) is defined as the ratio of highly liquid assets to current liabilities. It describes the minimum amount of highly liquid assets required to cover current liabilities within one trading day. The normative values of the coefficient H4 should be at least 20%. The current liquidity ratio (H5) is defined as the ratio of assets with residual maturities of up to 31 days to bank liabilities with residual maturities of up to 31 days. This ratio describes the minimum required amount of bank assets to enforce the current volume of liabilities within one calendar month. The normative values of the coefficient H5 should be at least 40%.

Short-term liquidity ratio (H6) is defined as the ratio of liquid assets to liabilities with residual maturities of one year. It determines the minimum required amount of assets to cover its liabilities for a period of one year. The normative values of the H6 ratio should be at least 60%.

Implementation of credit risk ratios by banks requires compliance with four indicators: maximum credit risk per counterparty (H7), large credit risks (H8), the maximum amount of loans, guarantees and warranties issued to one insider (H9), the maximum total amount of loans, guarantees and sureties issued to insiders (H10).

The maximum credit risk per counterparty (H7) is set to limit the credit risk arising from the failure of individual counterparties to meet their liabilities. The level of credit risk per counterparty is defined as the ratio of the amount of all obligations of the bank to this counterparty and all off-balance sheet liabilities of the bank to this counterparty (or a group of counterparties) to the bank's regulatory capital. The value of the H7 should be less than 25%.

The ratio of large credit risks (H8) is set to limit the concentration of credit risk by an individual counterparty or a group of related counterparties. The credit risk of the bank to a counterparty or to a group of related counterparties, is considered to be large, if the total of all requirements of the bank to this counterparty (or a group of related counterparties) and all off-balance sheet liabilities issued by the bank to this counterparty or group of related counterparties, is 10% of regulatory capital or more. H8 is defined as a ratio of all large credit risks, provided by the bank for all counterparties, taking into account all off-balance sheet commitments issued by the bank for these counterparties, to the bank's regulatory capital. The normative value of H8 should not exceed eight times the bank's regulatory capital.

The ratio of maximum amount of loans, guarantees and warranties issued to one insider (H9) is set to limit the risk arising from insider transactions that can lead to a direct or an indirect impact on the bank. H9 ratio is calculated as a ratio of all liabilities of the insider (or a group of related insiders) to the bank and all off-balance sheet commitments issued by the bank to this insider, and the share capital. The normative values of the coefficient H9 should not exceed 5%.

The ratio of the maximum total amount of loans and guarantees granted to insiders (H10) is set to limit the aggregate amount of risk on insiders. H10 ratio is calculated as a ratio of total debt liabilities to the bank of all insiders and 100% of the off-balance sheet liabilities issued by the Bank for all insiders to bank authorized capital. The normative values of the coefficient H10 should not exceed 30%.

The last group of indicators is ratios of investment, which are divided into the following indicators: investment in securities by each institution (H11), and total investment (H12). The ratio of investment in securities by each institution (H11) is set to limit the risk associated with investing in equities, shares and investment certificates of a separate legal entity. H11 ratio is defined as the ratio of the amount of funds invested on the purchase of shares (parts) and investment certificates separately by each institution to bank authorized capital. The normative values of H11 should not exceed 15%.

The ratio of total investment (H12) is set to limit the risks associated with the implementation of investment by the bank. H12 ratio is defined as the ratio of the amount of money invested on the purchase of shares (parts) and investment certificates of any legal entity to the authorized capital of the bank. The normative values of H12 should not exceed 60%.

The basis for the calculation of H2 H3, H7, H8, H11, and H12 is regulatory capital. It is authorized capital for the calculation of H9 and H10.

Based on the fact that systemically important banks in Ukraine have a significant impact on the banking system, certain other standards are applied to them. To determine the systemically important banks, the following indicators are used: total assets; funds of individuals, business entities and non-bank financial institutions; funds placed in other banks; funds raised from other banks; loans to entities in industry, agriculture and construction. The bank can be defined as systemically important if all indicators are higher than the arithmetic mean size indicator of the systemic importance of appropriate banks. This bank is obliged to adhere to specific values of economic requirements:

- liquidity ratios, including Instant liquidity ratio (H4) – at least 30%;
- credit risk ratios, including maximum credit risk per counterparty (H7) – no more than 20%.

If a systemically important bank obtained the status of a specialized bank, it must adhere to the values of the standards established for specialized banks.

Systemically important bank must also comply with the system importance buffer, which is calculated based on total risk.[96]

The branch of a foreign bank must carry out the following standards:
- sufficiency (adequacy) of regulatory capital;
- liquidity;
- credit risk;
- investment.

The monitoring of bank compliance of established economic requirements is implemented by the structural division of the National Bank, which is responsible for oversight of the bank on a regular basis. The calculation of a bank's (legal bodies) economic requirements is performed on the basis of daily balances as well as on the additional data.

At the same time, there are reports to show compliance with economic ratios, which are calculated in the following ways:

a) by daily calculations: ratios of the minimum regulatory capital of the bank (H1), the maximum credit risk per counterparty (H7), large credit risks (H8), the maximum credit risk on transactions with related parties of the bank (H9), instant liquidity ratio (H4);
b) by the weighted average formula (per month): investment in securities by each institution (H11), total investments (H12);
c) due on the 1–st, 11–th and 21–st days of each month: adequacy ratios (adequacy) of regulatory capital (H2), the capital adequacy (H3), current liquidity (H5), short-term liquidity (H6).

If off-site supervision or inspection find evidence of non-fulfillment of economic requirements by banks, appropriate sanctions will be applied to them, pursuant to Article 73 of the Law of Ukraine "On banks and banking activity" and relevant normative acts of the National Bank on application of enforcement measures.

The significant number of standards in banking regulation mechanism in Ukraine is due to the priority of maintaining the stability of financial intermediaries and the need for permanent reduction of bank risks in the Ukrainian financial system. However, these standards should be continually reviewed and revised (or eliminated) in parallel with the development of the banking system, because they place limitations on banks and their ability to actively use available capital.

96 The method for calculating economic standards of regulation of banks in Ukraine: Resolution of the NBU from 02.06.2009 # 315 – Access mode: http://zakon4.rada.gov.ua/laws/show/v0315500-09/page.

Another component of indicative regulations is the establishment of mandatory reservation – one of the monetary instruments for regulation of the money supply, management of money and the credit market. All cash, deposits and similar assets are subject to a mandatory reserve requirement, except for cash received from banks-residents, international financial organizations and cash received from the issuance of subordinated debt. The banks of Ukraine are subject to a mandatory reserve requirement for bank liabilities to the attracted money. Reserves are kept by the banks in Ukrainian national currency in their correspondent account of a bank in the National Bank of Ukraine and/or in a segregated account at the National bank of Ukraine.[97]

According to Resolution of the NBU Board from 18.12.2014 # 820 "On the change of order of forming and storage of mandatory reserves"[98] the determination of the amount of mandatory reserves for a particular period are set as following: the 11th day of a month is the first day of period of maintenance, and the 10th day of the next month is the closing date of the period of maintenance. The period of determination of reserve base is preceded to the period of maintenance of mandatory reserves, namely to the 11th day of each month.

Also, such norms of the mandatory reservation operate for forming of the banks' mandatory reserves:

- funds of deposit (deposits) of businesses and individuals in national and foreign currency on demand and money in current accounts–6.5%;
- term funds and deposit (deposits) of businesses and individuals in national and foreign currencies–3.0%.

The amount of the mandatory reserve, which should be maintained daily at the beginning of operational day on the correspondent account with the National Bank of Ukraine, should be at least 40% of the reserve base calculated for the relevant maintenance period. There is a limit on the number of bank's daily balance non-compliance cases of mandatory reserves held in correspondent accounts for three consecutive periods of retention.[99]

97 On approval of Instruction of regulation of Bank Activities in Ukraine: Resolution of the NBU from 28.08.2001 # 368 – Access mode: http://zakon5.rada.gov.ua/laws/show/z0841-01/page5.

98 On the change of order of forming and storage of mandatory reserves: Resolution of the NBU from 18.12.2014 # 820 – Access mode: http://zakon3.rada.gov.ua/laws/show/v0820500-14.

99 On Amendments to the Resolution of the Board of the National Bank of Ukraine from 18.12.2014 # 820: Resolution of the NBU from 17.03.2016 # 170 – Access mode: http://zakon3.rada.gov.ua/laws/show/v0170500-16/paran2#n2.

The next item of the indicative adjusting is establishment of norms of withholdings to reserves on coverage of risks from active bank transactions. According to the Regulation "On the definition credit risk from active banking operations by banks in Ukraine" from 30.06.2016 # 351, the bank defines credit risk for the following types of active operations:[100]

- loans to businesses and individuals;
- credits and requirements for banks (including reverse repo transactions, placing funds on correspondent accounts, funds in the calculations);
- financial receivables;
- receivables from economic activity;
- debt securities;
- shares and investments in other companies;
- derivative financial assets.

The bank calculates the credit risk of assets on an individual and group basis (Table 1).

Also, an integral part of the indicative adjusting is implementation of interest rate policy by NBU – adjusted by the National Bank for the demand and supply of monetary resources through the change of interest rates on the operations, targeting interest rates in money and credit market as well as the yield of financial operations. With the aim of setting interest rate policy, the NBU sets the following interest rates:

1) discount rate;
2) standing facilities;
3) on the deposit certificates;
4) on loans for refinancing.

The decision regarding the discount rate is determined by the Board of the National Bank of Ukraine at a meeting on monetary policy on the basis of the proposals from the Department of Monetary Policy and Economic Analysis after discussions at the Committee monetary policy meeting. Within instruments of permanent access, NBU sets a corridor of the interest rates on the granting and withdrawal of liquidity for the overnight period (on overnight loans and certificates of deposit overnight) to control short-term interest rates in the interbank market by limiting fluctuations around their discount rate. The limits of the interest rate corridor are symmetrical with respect to the discount rate and in case of change vary on the same amount. The interest rate on overnight loans is set at the level of the discount rate plus two percentage

100 On the definition credit risk from active banking operations by banks in Ukraine: Resolution of the NBU from 30.06.2016 # 351 – Access mode: http://zakon3.rada.gov.ua/laws/show/v0351500-16.

TABLE 1 Definition of credit risk on active operations[a]

| The level of credit risk on active operations | |
|---|---|
| On individual base | On group base |
| $CR_{iH\partial} = \max\left\{0; PD\times\left[EAD-\left(\sum_{i=1}^{j}(CV\times k)i+RC\right)\right]\right\}$ | $CR_{зрун} = \sum_{m=1}^{n} EAD_m \times PD_{зрун} \times LGD_{зрун}$ |
| that is based on the formula:<br>$CR_{iH\partial} = PD_{iH\partial} \times LGD_{iH\partial} \times EAD_{iH\partial}$<br>where $CR_{інд}$ – level of credit risk on asset on individual base;<br>$PD_{інд}$ – coefficient of probability of default of borrower/counterparty by the asset that is defined by bank according to Regulation;<br>$LGD_{iH\partial} = 1 - RR_{iH\partial}$<br>where $RR_{інд}$ – coefficient that demonstrates the level of debt repayment by asset due to implementation of guarantee and other income,<br>$RR_{iH\partial} = \left(\sum_{i=1}^{j}(CV\times k)i+RC\right) / EAD_{iH\partial}$<br>$EAD_{інд}$ – exposition of risk by the asset at the estimation date;<br>$CV_i$ – cost of *i* type of guarantee that is counted according to the credit risk level (in case of several types of guarantee by one asset),<br>$k_i$ – coefficient of liquidity of *i* type of guarantee. According to the prevailing opinions on the amount of costs of the guarantee, bank applies the lower (smaller) values of liquidity provision;<br>RC – other incomes, in particular indemnity, financial guarantee, the realization of the debtor's property / property guarantor, except pledged | where $CR_{груп}$ – level of credit risk on group of financial assets;<br>n – total amount of credits in the group of financial assets;<br>m – sequence number of credit in the group of financial assets;<br>EAD – exposition of risk at the estimation date;<br>$PD_{груп}$ – coefficient of probability of default of borrower/counterparty, included to the group of financial assets, defined according to Regulation;<br>$LGD_{груп}$ – coefficient that corresponds to the level of costs by group of financial assets in case of default defined according to Regulation |

a The definition of risk of the banking institutions according the using of its services for the legalization of criminal income or financing of terrorism during the inspection: monograph / [Dmitrov S. O., Medvid T. A., Levchenko L. G., Butkovskaya T. P., Kuzmenko O. V. and others]; under the General editorship of O. M. Berezhnoy. – Sumy: "Ukrainian Academy of banking of the NBU", 2014. – 103 p

points, and the overnight deposit certificates is set at the level of the discount rate minus two percentage points.

With refinancing loans granted by tender to support banks, the National Bank sets the interest rate and the marginal interest rate on refinancing credits to maintain a banks' liquidity at the level of interest rates on overnight loans.

Also within the indicative regulation by the NBU, refinancing is carried out: on operations with banks to provide loans, whose main purpose is to regulate bank liquidity to perform central control functions of lender of last resort.

For this purpose, the National Bank uses the following loans:

- permanent refinancing credit line to provide banks with overnight loans (on the following terms: the collateral of government bonds of Ukraine (except bonds of external state loan) or overnight deposit facilities;
- refinancing loans for up to 90 days.

Furthermore, if liquidity support to banks for a longer term is necessary, the National Bank of Ukraine may decide to refinance through advances for up to 360 days.

Refinancing of banks comes through conducting quantitative or interest rate liquidity-providing advances. They are held at the following frequency: 3 Wednesdays in a row – up to 14 days, and one Wednesday – up to 90 days.

NBU makes bank refinancing through advances only under the appropriate secured measures which should be communicated to the banks on a quarterly basis.

The types of assets (property) eligible as a collateral for refinancing loans can be the following:

- government bonds of Ukraine (domestic state bonds of Ukraine, government bonds of Ukraine, target government bonds of Ukraine);
- certificates of deposit;
- foreign currency (US Dollar, Euro, Pound Sterling, Swiss Francs, Japanese Yen);
- bonds of international financial organizations.

The National Bank of Ukraine refinances bank advances or loans at an interest rate not lower than the discount rate of the National Bank of Ukraine, which during the loan agreement shall not be changed.[101]

Other essential items of indicative regulation are maintaining correspondent relationships as well as maintaining reserves, transactions in the open

101 On the application of the National bank of Ukraine standard instruments regulating banking system liquidity: Resolution of the NBU from 17.09.2015 # 615 – Access mode: http://zakon5.rada.gov.ua/laws/show/v0615500-15.

market and the export and import of currency. The correspondent relationships with NBU means entering into a commercial bank agreement for transaction settlement and the provision of cash services by opening correspondent accounts. It is intended to reflect the calculation, which is carried out by a bank on behalf and at the expense of another bank on the basis of a signed correspondent agreement between them (contract).[102]

Foreign exchange reserves are reflected on the balance sheet of NBU, combining certain assets and international currencies accepted for international payments. In order to ensure internal and external stability of Ukraine, NBU has foreign exchange reserves, which consist of the following assets:

- gold;
- special drawing rights;
- reserve position in the IMF;
- foreign currency in the form of banknotes and coins or funds on accounts abroad;
- securities (other than shares), which are paid in foreign currency;
- any other internationally recognized reserve assets.

Management of foreign exchange reserves by NBU assumes these reserves will be replenished and used to achieve the following objectives:

1) sale of foreign currency in the financial markets for monetary policy, including exchange rate policy;
2) expenses of foreign exchange transactions, monetary metals and other internationally recognized reserve assets and operations with the support of the National Bank in the estimated amounts of revenues and expenses provided by the NBU;
3) repayment of by the NBU in foreign exchange funds to international financial institutions, foreign central banks and other lenders, including interest on such funds and other compulsory charges;
4) participation in the formation of capital and activities of international organizations.[103]

Open market operations through the purchase or sale of treasury bills of the National Bank of Ukraine and other securities (other than securities confirming corporate rights) and such as debt instruments as defined by the Board of the National Bank to regulate the money market, improve interbank transactions

102 Mishchenko V. I. (2007) Banking operations: Textbook – Kyiv. – Pp. 177 – 205.

103 On the National Bank of Ukraine: Law of Ukraine from 20.05.1999 # 679-XIV. – Access mode: http://zakon2.rada.gov.ua/laws/show/679-14.

in securities and to promote market price quotations for the public bonds of issued by Ukraine.[104]

Regulation of import and export of capital is an instrument of influence on the money supply in circulation, implemented by the National Bank through the following actions:

- registration of the import and export of capital;
- setting maximum and minimum interest rates on foreign deposits in Ukrainian banks;
- establishing for entities who are in debt to non-residents, mandatory non-interest investments of a certain amount of debt for authorized banks in Ukraine.[105]

Thus, an indicative form of the regulation of banks consists of a wide range of components of regulation and oversight on individual banks and the banking system to achieve economic stability.

Against this background, it is important to emphasize that state regulation and supervision of the banking system are executed by the NBU through its different departments assigned with specific regulatory powers (Figure 8).

NBU is in possession of an arsenal of a vast number of diverse instruments for banking regulation. Nevertheless, their effectiveness is questionable because of the critical situation of Ukraine's financial system. The implementation of European standards of banking regulation in the Ukrainian banking sector, in addition to the existence of national restrictions, has led to significant overregulation of the banking system and to the existence of unequal opportunities for different banks. At the same time, numerous regulations by the NBU, and its active participation in the regulatory process requirements of banks, has not provided for a stable functioning banking system. This leads to the need to review the concept of regulation of banks in Ukraine and to continue qualitative reforms of the structure of the NBU.

## 3 The EU-Ukraine Association Agreement and Its Implications on Ukrainian Banking Regulation

The EU-Ukraine Action Plan negotiations on a new enhanced regulatory agreement, which replaces the previous Cooperation and Partnership

104 On the application of the National bank of Ukraine standard instruments regulating banking system liquidity: Resolution of the NBU from 17.09.2015 # 615 – Access mode: http://zakon5.rada.gov.ua/laws/show/v0615500-15.

105 Moroz A. M. (2005) The Central Bank and monetary policy: Textbook – Kyiv: KNEU. – 556 p.

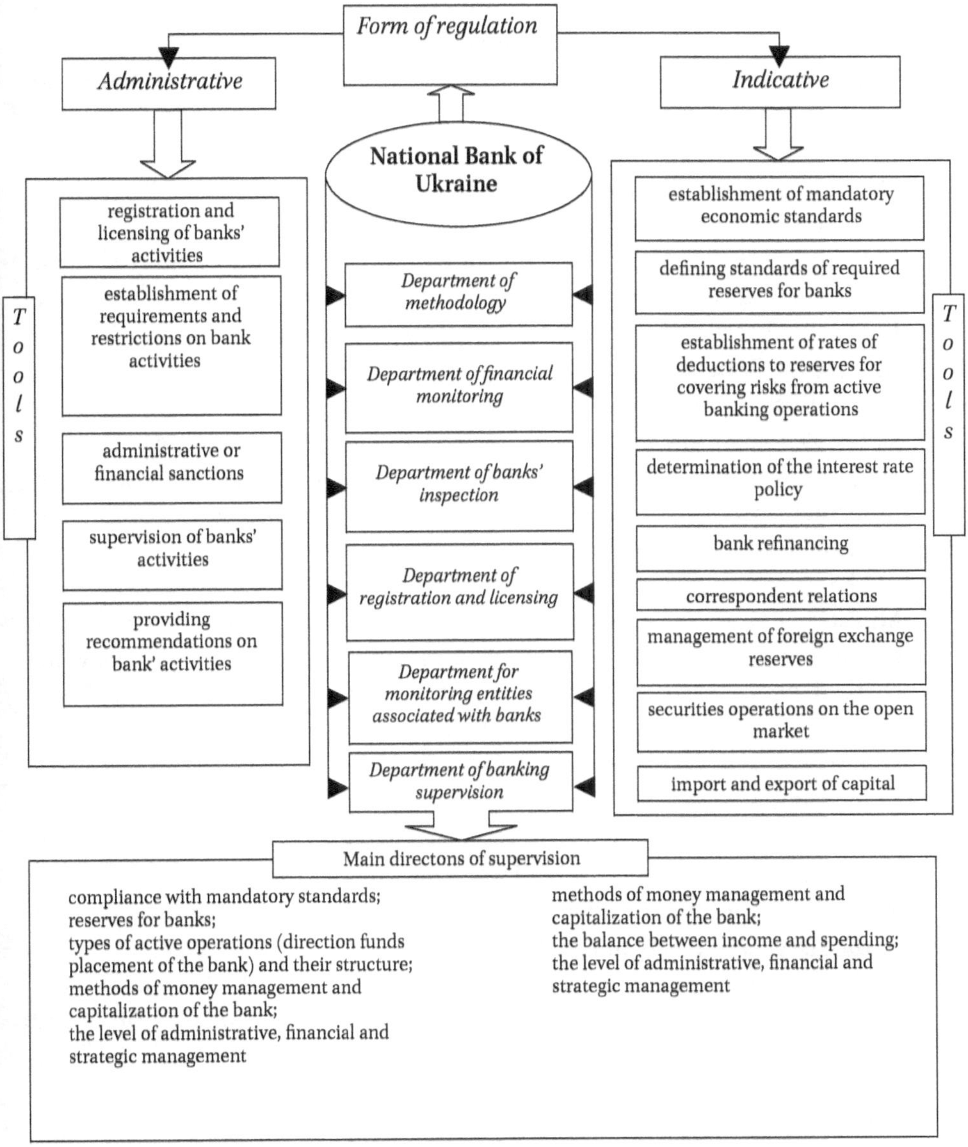


FIGURE 8 The mechanism of state regulation and supervision of banking system

Agreement, began in March 2007. In September 2008, EU-Ukraine Summit took place in Paris, which created an understanding to work on a more comprehensive agreement between the EU and Ukraine. This served as the basis for the EU-Ukraine Association Agreement. Between 2007–2012, twenty-one rounds of negotiations regarding this Association Agreement were held, with the majority (19) concentrating on the "Deep and Comprehensive Free Trade Area" chapter.

Conclusions of the discussions regarding the EU-Ukraine Association Agreement were set out in 19 December 2011 at the next EU-Ukraine Summit. The Association Agreement was much more comprehensive in comparison to its predecessors and is clearly intended to strengthen the overall EU-Ukrainian relationship. After its approval, the Association Agreement was signed on 20 March 2012. In addition to this, the "Deep and Comprehensive Free Trade Area" chapter was signed on 19 July 2012.

From late 2012 until mid-2013, the translation of the Association Agreement into the official languages of the EU and Ukraine took place. Furthermore, the EU Council received recommendations from the European Commission to sign the Agreement and to ensure the continuation of its provisional application until the procedures of ratification were completed by all EU Member States. The publication of the official draft of the Association Agreement was made on 9 August 2013 under the official and final title being "Association Agreement between the European Union and it Member States, of the one part, and Ukraine, of the other part".

The Association Agreement was signed in two stages. First, the Prime Minister of Ukraine signed the Final Act and political part on March 21, 2014 during the respective EU-Ukraine Summit. More specifically, the following parts of the Association Agreement had been signed: The Preamble, Title I "General Principles", Title II "Political dialogue and reform association, cooperation and convergence in foreign and security policy", Title VII "Institutional, general and final provisions.

Second, on 27 June 2014, EU leaders, including the European Council, the Heads of State and Heads of the Government of the 28 EU member states as well as the President of Ukraine were signing the economic part of the Association Agreement. This included Title III "Justice, Freedom and Security", Title IV "Trade and trade-related matters", Title V "Economic and sector cooperation" and Title VI "financial cooperation and anti-fraud provisions". Consequently both – the political part and the economic part – are the pillars of the Association Agreement.

On 16 September 2014, both the European Parliament and the Ukrainian Parliament approved the Association Agreement. Reflecting its broad scope, the Association Agreement can be considered as the longest legal document in Ukrainian history as well as the longest document, which was ever concluded between the EU and a third country. The Association Agreement is essential for the establishment of a new format for the relationship between the EU and Ukraine, leading to an enhanced economic integration and political association. Moreover, the Association Agreement provides for some strategic guidelines "for systematic socio-economic reforms in Ukraine".

Ultimately, the EU-Ukraine Association Agreement came into force on 1 November 2014.[106] According to Art 1 of the Association Agreement, its main goals are the following:

1. Enhance gradual reconciliation between the Parties, which will be based on the mutual values and privileged and closed interconnections;
2. Provide suitable legal background for mutual political dialogue in all areas of common interest between the Parties;
3. Improve, encourage and preserve stability and peace in the international as well as regional magnitudes, according to the "Helsinki Final Act of 1975 of the Conference on the Security and Cooperation in Europe", "the United Nation Charter" and "the Charter of Paris for a new Europe of 1990";
4. Establish an environment for heightened trade and economic relations, which will lead to full integration of Ukraine into the European Union Internal Market (including the establishment of" the Deep and Comprehensive Free Trade Area", as it is stated in Title VI of the Association Agreement) and to encourage attempts of Ukraine to complete convergence into well-functioning market economy, by means of the aligning and accepting appropriate regulations of the Union;
5. Improve collaboration in the areas of Freedom, Security, and Justice, with an intention of reinforcement the rule of law and to strengthening fundamental freedoms and human rights;
6. Settle confident conditions in order to intensify close cooperation between the Parties in other areas of common interest.

Given the broad scope of the Association Agreement, it takes a while to find Title VI "Trade and Trade Related Matters", Chapter 6, Sub-section 6, which is dedicated to financial services. In this respect, Art 125 provides a definition of financial services, which includes insurance and insurance related services, as well as banking and other financial services.

Banking and financial services include deposits taking and other repayable reserves from the public; all lending types, including financing of commercial transactions, consumer and mortgage credits; financial leasing; commitments and guarantees; different types of trading (for the customer and for own account of the financial institution); all payments and money transmissions; participation in the issuance, underwriting and placement of all types of the financial instruments; money brokering; transfer and provision of financial

106 Government Portal. (2015, December 24). Association Agreement between the European Union and Ukraine: http://www.kmu.gov.ua/control/en/publish/article%3Fart_id=248279225&cat_id=248274610.

information; asset management; clearing and settlement for financial assets; intermediation, advisory and other financial services.

Art 126 "Prudential carve-out" stresses that each Party should maintain or adopt procedures for investor protection, and ensure the stability and integrity of the Party's financial system. Moreover, under Art. 127, which is devoted to Effective and Transparent Regulation, it is stated, that all Parties ought to make their best efforts in order to ensure implementation of all internationally established standards for the supervision and regulation of the financial sector as well as limiting tax avoidance and evasion fight.

The following internationally established and agreed standards are the following:

- the Basel Committee's "Core Principle for Effective Banking Supervision",
- the International Association of Insurance supervisors "Insurance Core Principles",
- the International Organization of Securities Commissions' "Objectives and principles of Security Regulation",
- the OECD's "Agreement on exchange of information on tax matters",
- the G-20 "Statement on Transparency and Exchange of information for tax purposes" and
- the Financial Action Task Force's "Forty Recommendations on Money Laundering" and "Nine Recommendations on Terrorist Financing".

Moreover, Art 133 "Regulatory approximation" describes the importance of conforming the former Ukrainian legislation to the EU level which requires Ukraine to ensure that all its former and future legislation will be comparable with EU law. This process has been started from the date of the ratification of the Association Agreement.[107]

Financial services are addressed in Title V "Economic and Sector Cooperation", Chapter 12 of the Association Agreement. Art 383 claims that an effective set of rules and regulation in financial services is needed in order to foster trade exchanges between the Parties as well as to ensure a full-functioning market economy. Consequently, the Parties agreed to support the process of conforming the relevant regulations in the area of financial services. Moreover, a clear focus of the Association Agreement is on investor and consumer protection in financial services as well as on the integrity and stability of the global financial system. Cooperation among different actors, including supervisors and regulators of the financial system, should consequently be promoted. It was mutually agreed that an effective independent supervisory system needs to be established. It was also agreed, that all Parties should promote cooperation

107 Association Agreement between the European Union and its Member States, of the one part, and Ukraine, of the other part. (2014, November 1).

among relevant supervisory authorities as well as regulatory bodies, including the sharing of an expertise and information. In addition, Art. 385 claims, that all parties should minimize the gap between existing regulations and recognize international standards in the areas of financial regulation and financial supervision.[108]

From a business perspective, the Association Agreement is also a reflection of the fact that the EU remains the largest donor to the Ukraine with financial support having been accumulated to as much as EUR 2,5 billion since 1991. EUR 470 million were allocated to Ukraine between 2011–2013 under the so-called "European Neighborhood Policy Instrument", which strives to support the rule of law, the promotion of an Association Agreement as well as appropriate development measures, with a special focus on the areas of environment and energy as well as good governance.[109]

Ukraine is benefiting from EU financial support, which is done through funding instruments and mechanisms, which should contribute to the achievement of the goals and objectives of the Association Agreement. EU financial assistance is governed by the "EU Financial Instrument Regulations", which cover relevant programs that are established to transmit financial support to the agreed areas, thereby satisfying Ukrainian needs. Against this background, it is intended to make best use of the available resources, which requires close coordination and cooperation between the parties. In any case, any donor to Ukraine as well as any international financial institution has to act in accordance with the "international principles of aid effectiveness".[110] In order to enhance the better coordination and operation in the area of financial services, a transition to EU standards, as well as institutional changes to the Ukrainian financial services industry, are necessary. Thus, the Association Agreement is providing a list and timetable regarding the implementation of relevant EU Directives and provisions into Ukrainian law.

Parts of "Directive 2006/48/EC of the European Parliament and of the Council", which governs the business of the financial institutions, have to be adopted. Table 2 provides the required timeframe for the implementation, as well as the specific provisions, which need to be adopted by Ukraine.

---

108 Association Agreement between the European Union and its Member States, of the one part, and Ukraine, of the other part. (2014, November 1).

109 European Commission. (n.d.). EU-Ukraine Association Agreement "Guide to the Association Agreement". Retrieved from European Commission: http://eeas.europa.eu/archives/docs/images/top_stories/140912_eu-ukraine-associatin-agreement-quick_guide.pdf.

110 Association Agreement between the European Union and its Member States, of the one part, and Ukraine, of the other part. (2014, November 1).

TABLE 2 Timetable for application of the directive 2006/48/EC provisions

| Expected progress in adoption of EU regulation for credit institutions | Applicable provisions of Directive 2006/48/EC | Expected timeframe for implementation |
|---|---|---|
| Requirements for the access to the taking up and pursuit of the business of credit institutions | Title II | 4 years |
| Relations with third countries | Title IV | 4 years |
| Principals for prudential supervision | Title V Chapter 1 Section 2–3 | 4 years |
| Definition of own funds | Title V Chapter 2 Section 1 | 4 years |
| Large exposures provisions | Title V Chapter 2 Section 5 | 4 years |
| Provisions against risk accordance with Basel I:<br>– Capital requirements for credit risk<br>– Capital requirements for position risk, settlement and counterparty risk, FX and commodity risk<br>– Excluding the application of Article 123 and Title V chapter 5, namely the supervisory review process and disclosure requirements | Title V Chapter 2 Section 2 | 4 years |
| Remaining provisions of the Directive (in accordance with Basel II) especially:<br>– Capital requirements for credit risk<br>– Capital requirements for operational risk<br>– Capital requirements for position risk, settlement and counterparty risk, FX and commodity risk<br>– Application of Article 123 and Title V chapter 5, namely the supervisory review process and disclosure requirements<br>Title V Chapter 4 on supervision | | 6 years |

SOURCE: "ASSOCIATION AGREEMENT BETWEEN THE EUROPEAN UNION AND IT MEMBER STATES, OF THE ONE PART, AND UKRAINE, OF THE OTHER PART", APPENDIX XVII-2.

In addition to this, the norms regarding procedural rules or the credit quality assessment of acquisitions in the financial sector, has to be enforced within six years after the signing of the Association Agreement. Some provisions of Directive 2006/49/EC on the capital adequacy of investment firms and credit institutions have to be implemented within four years after the signing of the Association Agreement. Directive 94/19/EC on the deposit-guaranteed schemes also has to be implemented within four years after the signing of the Association Agreement. Furthermore, "Directive 86/635/EEC of 8 December 1986 on the annual accounts and consolidated accounts of banks and other financial institutions", needs to be implemented in 4 years as well. Moreover, Ukraine needs to conform its legislation pursuant to EU Directives and the respective provisions regarding the rules of valuations for consolidated and annual accounts for certain types of companies, including financial institutions and banks.[111]

From a structural point of view, Ukraine is employing a two-tier banking system. NBU is the regulatory and supervisory body and commercial banks are the respective economic agents. Officially, NBU is considered as an independent entity; nevertheless there is evidence indicating that improvements in this respect are necessary. Although Ukraine, in principle, applies internationally agreed standards, such as Basel II and Basel III, it still lacks a proper supervisory framework. At the end of 2014, the number of licensed banks was 165, involving 51 banks with holdings of foreign capital; whereas the amount of the foreign capital in the Ukrainian banking system decreased to 32,2% in comparison to 2012 with significant 41,9%.

The stability of the Ukrainian Banking system also significantly weakened during 2014. The level of adequacy of regulatory capital was only equal to 14%, which is considered as the lowest since the GFC in 2007/8. Banks were reporting a 14,6% share of non-preforming loans, which is approximately a 2% increase compared to 2103. Equity and returns on assets were also reported as negative. The continuing outflows of deposits also had a negative impact on the stability of the banking system.[112] Consequently, the signing of the Association Agreement triggered a necessary wave of reforms in the Ukrainian financial sector with the expectation that the adoption of EU standards will

111 Association Agreement between the European Union and its Member States, of the one part, and Ukraine, of the other part. (2014, November 1).

112 BTI. (2016). Ukraine Country Report. Bertelsmann Stiftung's Transformation Index. Bertelsmann Stiftung.

lead to structural stabilization and regulatory strengthening of the Ukrainian financial sector.[113]

The harmonization process of Ukraine towards EU standards puts NBU into a leading role since one of its major tasks is concerned with ensuring that the Ukrainian financial system is gradually conformed to EU standards and rules. In this respect, NBU was actively taking part in the process culminating in the signing of the Association Agreement. It also put forward a draft of the Action Plan for the implementation of the Association Agreement which was accepted by the Ordinance of the Cabinet of Ministers of Ukraine #847–p from 17 September 2104. The Cabinet guaranteed to take all the necessary measures laid out in this plan.

In 2014, NBU continued to establish bilateral international collaborations with other central banks. This was done to widen its international network and to ensure the proper development of the Ukrainian banking sector by improving the reputation of Ukraine in order to stimulate more foreign investments.

In 2014, the Public Council was established by NBU to serve as a communication platform to facilitate collaboration between the general public and NBU. It intends to ensure the protection of the interests and rights of investors and any other users of banking services. The Public Council was established by NBU Resolution #335, from June 5, 2014 and is the first of this kind in Ukrainian history. It consists of 15 members, which rotate every two years. From a material point of view, the following topics are to be addressed by the Public Council:

- foreign currency loans,
- insolvent banks,
- payments to individuals,
- reforms of the banking system and
- stabilization of hryvnia.[114]

Although NBU plays a crucial role in the transformation process as mentioned, the NBU was reorganized in order to improve its competencies and effectiveness as regulator. NBU's reorganization process started at the end of 2014 and was conducted in three stages: During the first stage (2014–2015) the analysis of the existing structure was completed. The second stage (2015–2016) was dedicated to the introduction and implementation of the new organizational structure of the NBU and the third stage (2016–2017) reflected the changes in the structure of the regional offices. The main focus of the overall

113 National Bank of Ukraine. (2016, July 14). Financial sector reform: https://bank.gov.ua/control/en/publish/article?art_id=33820082&cat_id=33820081.

114 NBU internal transformation / National Bank of Ukraine – Access mode: https://bank.gov.ua/control/en/publish/article?art_id=24761917&cat_id=24761916.

reorganization is the reduction of the hierarchical levels of the regional offices as well as at NBU in general, by centralizing management tasks and improving the setup of NBU's. In addition, all internal processes of the NBU are subject to this major reorganization.

During this reorganization, NBU has been actively working on the implementation of Directive 2006/48/EC, as laid out in the Association Agreement, and had received an extended mandate to supervise and monitor not only the activities of banking groups, but also those of non-banking financial institutions. This technical work can be seen by the introduction of the new concept of independent directors, which was introduced in Ukraine by NBU. In this context, a set of regulations was established regarding restrictions on transactions with the management board and insiders of a bank. These measures also introduced reporting requirements to NBU in order to improve its oversight.

Aside from improved banking supervision, Ukraine is also obliged to implement new requirements regarding the solvency and capital adequacy requirements of other financial institutions according to Basel III. This is necessary, since the Ukrainian banking system – to a substantial extent – is still operating on the basis of Basel I. Consequently, a transition phase through 2020 should help to bring Ukrainian banks in compliance with the respective laws of NBU[115] based on EU standards such as Resolution #312 from May 12, 2015 "On Amendments to the Instruction on Banking Regulation in Ukraine".

According to the new requirements, as of the beginning of 2019, the capital adequacy ratio for all Ukrainian banks should at least be 7%.[116] However, according to the "Comprehensive Program of Ukraine Financial Sector Development", the capital adequacy ratio of the banking system is planned to be more than 10% and will thus satisfy the requirements of Basel III.[117] Moreover, additional buffers should be created over the Tier 1 capital adequacy ratio, which will allow banks to overcome its distressed market environment and to decrease the probability of default. The respective introduction of such capital buffers is planned for 2020.

115 Borodkin A. (2015) (Sisetska A., Nikolenko O. (n.d.)) Ukraine. In the Banking Regulation Review (Vol. 6). London, United Kingdom: Gideon Roberton.

116 National Bank of Ukraine. (2015, May 15). The National Bank of Ukraine announces introduction of new bank capital requirements as well as specific requirements to systemically important banks: https://bank.gov.ua/control/en/publish/printable_article;jsessionid=F29ECD19093B1A289F989E39627405C1?art_id=17537282&showTitle=true.

117 National Bank of Ukraine Board Resolution. (2015, June 18). Comprehensive program of Ukraine Financial sector development until 2020: https://bank.gov.ua/doccatalog/document?id=43401314.

In this context it is also worth mentioning that the banks should accumulate conservation buffers during the economic growth to counterbalance potential losses during the recession time. As it was outlined by the Basel Committee on Banking Supervision, conservation buffer will start from 0,625% and increase to 2,5% during 2020–2023. Moreover, a countercyclical buffer is also required and proposed to defend the banking system from the accumulated risks during the time of credit deficit. The size of the buffer will depend on the phase of economic development and vary between 0% to 2,5%.

Special requirements were established by NBU for systematically important financial institutions, which makes NBU also follow an international regulatory trend. Systematically important financial institutions should maintain the instant liquidity ratio of 30% and single party exposure should not exceed 20%. Moreover, systemic importance buffer should be held by such institution, starting from 1 January 2020. The size of such buffer will be set in a range of 1% to 2%, depending on the size of the institution.[118]

On 11 March 2015, by the order of the "NBU Governor On Establishment of the financial Sector Reforms Task Force", a new distinct executive body, which is responsible for the development and implementation of financial sector reforms in Ukraine, had been established. It consists of regulators of financial markets, the Ukrainian Ministry of Finance, the Deposit Guaranteed Fund, NBU, the Secretariat of the Parliamentary Committee on Finance and Banking, representatives of the business community and other experts.

The major achievement of this body is the development of the Comprehensive Program of Ukrainian Financial Sector Development Until 2020. Under this program, all Ukrainian obligations from the Association Agreement should be addressed by ensuring the creation of a well-functioning financial sector according to EU standards. In order to meet this objective, the program is addressing three main areas:

- investor protection and other financial markets consumers;
- growth of the institutional capability of the regulators of financial markets;
- guaranteeing financial stability and development of the Ukrainian financial sector.[119]

118 National Bank of Ukraine. (2015, May 15). The National Bank of Ukraine announces introduction of new bank capital requirements as well as specific requirements to systemically important banks: https://bank.gov.ua/control/en/publish/printable_article;jsessionid=F29ECD19093B1A289F989E39627405C1?art_id=17537282&showTitle=true.

119 National Bank of Ukraine. (n.d.a). Comprehensive Program of Ukrainian Financial Sector Development Until 2020. Retrieved from National Bank of Ukraine: https://bank.gov.ua/control/en/publish/article?art_id=33820088&cat_id=33820087. Moreover, see National

According to the Association Agreement, Ukraine should implement Directive 94/19/EC from May 30, 1994 on the Deposit Guaranteed Schemes into national law. The European Union has replaced this act by the Directive 2014/49/EC from 16 April 2014. This new Directive serves as the basis for the restructuring of deposit guarantee schemes in Ukraine,[120] which is reflected in the law of Ukraine "On Amendment of Some Legislative Acts of Ukraine in Respect of the Improvement of the Household Deposit Guarantee System and the Resolution of Insolvent Banks" which entered into force on 12 September 2015.

The most significant material aspects of this law are the attempts to strengthen the Deposit Guarantee Fund (DGF) authority regarding the administration and liquidation of distressed banks, which is also reflected by new intervention powers of DGF. Furthermore, any property of such a bank can only be sold in the form of open tenders or auctions.[121] Moreover, DGF has continued to develop its policy decisions, which are, for example, reflected in the second stage of its development, which focused on the resolution- and decision-making process regarding failed banks. In this respect, the time for approval of the resolution plan for a distorted bank was reduced to 30 days. Also the term for temporary bank administration was shortened to one month, with an option of extension with an aim to implement a resolution plan.[116]

All these activities reflect Ukraine's willingness to actively transform its financial sector and regulatory environment towards EU standards. According to NBU (2016), more than twenty-one drafts of financial reforms were proposed for parliamentary approval by concentrating on the areas of consumer and credit rights protection, restructuring of the corporate and foreign currency denominated debt as well as merging state regulations regarding the financial markets. Consequently, Draft Law No. 2456–d "On Amendments to Certain Legal Acts of Ukraine in Respect of the Improvement of Financial Services Consumer Rights protection", which passed the first reading on 31 March 2016, aims to tackle inconsistences regarding the laws and regulations of consumer protection and to establish a proper legal framework for regulation of the relationship between banks, individuals and other financial institutions according to EU standards. It states, that financial institutions should be liable for not providing in time or at all relevant information regarding the financial services, required by law.

---

Bank of Ukraine. (n.d.a). Task Force on Reforms: https://bank.gov.ua/control/en/publish/article?art_id=33820110&cat_id=33820109.

120 National Bank of Ukraine. (2016). Financial stability Report.

121 Deposit Guarantee Fund. (2105, February 16). Retrieved from Deposit Guarantee Fund: http://www.fg.gov.ua/en/.

This draft is setting out a framework for information disclosure, by a bank and non-bank institutions and claims, that the minimum amount of the information to be disclosed should be defined by the NBU. Since there is no separate law on the protection of creditors and consumers, the Draft Law No. 2455 "On Consumer Lending" proposes a separation of laws as most European countries employ. Draft Law No. 2286–a "On Amendments to Certain Legal Acts of Ukraine on the Restoration of Trust Between Borrowers and Lenders" was rejected by the Parliament on 13 April 2016. It aimed to decrease existing loopholes, which were typically used by the debtors for their obligations fulfillment.

Another example worth mentioning is Draft No. 2413–a "On Amendments to Certain Legal Acts of Ukraine on the Consolidation of the State Regulation of Financial Markets Functions" which was proposed and approved on the first reading in the Ukrainian Parliament. The main idea is to divide the functions of the National Commission for State Regulation of Financial Services Markets among the National Security, the Stock Market Commission, and NBU. This will contribute to a greater transparency of the regulations of financial markets, as well as will increase confidence in the financial services from the consumer perspective.[122]

The law "On Financial Restructuring" #1414-VII came into force on 14 June 2016 and can be understood as a measure to decrease the volumes of non-performing loans. The law is aiming to facilitate a restructuring of debt out-of-court for the truthful debtors, which are at the early phase of distress. Thus, a comprehensive restructuring regime is created. It encourages foreign and domestic debtors to arrange a discussion platform with borrowers. Particularly, the law is dealing with statutory memorandums; grace periods; organizing a committee for lender coordination; development and implementation of the restructuring plan, which should be agreed by all parties involved.[123]

Resolution #351 of 20 June 2016, which was established by NBU, provides a new methodology for credit risk assessment, which complies with the Basel principles and IFRS 9. This resolution should enter into force on 1 January 2018 and is accompanied by clear and detailed guidelines regarding the assessment of credit risk in order to ensure that banks and regulators make a rational

122 National Bank of Ukraine. (2016). Financial draft laws. Retrieved from National Bank of Ukraine: https://bank.gov.ua/control/en/publish/article?art_id=33868732&cat_id=33868731.

123 Kurdydyk O. (2016) (Pshenychniuk D., Sverdlov I.) Ukrainian financial restructuring: new consensual work-outs for distressed business came into force on 19 October 2016 / DLA Piper. Access mode: https://www.dlapiper.com/en/ukraine/insights/publications/2016/10/ukrainian-financial-restructuring/.

judgment regarding the quality of assets. However, the application of the new principles for the credit risk assessment has been in force since 3 January 2017.[124]

Moreover, NBU has authorized short-term FX securities as eligible investments and simplified the procedure for banks to purchase highly liquid debt securities. Furthermore, the maturity of an instrument should not be more than five years. Purchase of foreign debt instruments will increase the number of high quality assets, which will be beneficial for the liquidity management under the of Basel III requirements, specifically for the liquidity coverage ratio implementation.[125]

A new law on consumer lending was adopted by the Parliament of Ukraine on 15 November 2016. This introduces new requirements for consumer loan advertisement and prohibits the usage of some marketing techniques. This will likely lead to drastic changes in the consumer lending market since it stresses the importance of creditworthiness. Lenders should conduct a creditworthiness assessment of the borrower before entering a loan contract. Moreover, lenders should provide the borrower with a written conformation about the timeline of payments, the amounts which to be paid and the part of the loan, which remains outstanding. The requirements for establishing a loan agreement are also included in order to balance loan contract conditions for borrower protection. Thus, it should lead to the prevention of unfair practices, which have happened in Ukraine. Consequently, the adoption of this legislation is an important step towards the creation of a transparent and competitive market for consumer lending.[126] According to the amendments to the "Certain Laws of Ukraine on Indemnity to Individuals under Individual Deposits through the Deposit Guarantee System for Damage Caused by Abuses in the Banking and other Financial Services", Ukrainian banks are prohibited from taking consumer deposits and instantaneously making loans from the proceeds without properly registering it on the bank's balance sheet. However, banks are legally allowed to perform P2P lending, which is considered as an intermediary function.[127]

---

124 National Bank of Ukraine. (2016, June 4). The National Bank of Ukraine changed the approach to credit risk assessment by banks: https://bank.gov.ua/control/en/publish/printable_article;jsessionid=7C60BD4F398A5D199796155DE4525CED?art_id=32898626&showTitle=true.

125 National Bank of Ukraine. (2016). Finacial stability Report. National Bank of Ukraine.

126 Ukraine: law on consumer lending adopted (2016) / CMS Law-Now. Access mode: http://www.cms-lawnow.com/ealerts/2016/11/ukraine-law-on-consumer-lending-adopted.

127 National Bank of Ukraine. (2016). Financial stability Report. National Bank of Ukraine.

Moreover, DGF also covers investor deposits since 1 January2017.[128] NBU is currently working on a strategy for macro-prudential supervision and banking resolution, which will be in line with the respective EU requirements, including the establishment of Emergency Liquidity Assistance, which is also covered by NBU's mandate.

As these examples demonstrate, Ukraine is working hard to improve its regulatory and supervisory framework in the areas of financial services in order to be in line with EU (and international) standards. Consequently, the Association Agreement should be considered as the key trigger to stimulate these developments. Nevertheless, it is important to point out, that the current Ukrainian ambition is not necessarily reflective of a clear and consistent strategy, which means that the ultimate success of the ambitious Ukrainian efforts in this respect remains to be seen.

## 4 Financial Monitoring

Financial monitoring has become one of the main components of a comprehensive implementation of banking supervision not only in Ukraine but worldwide. International and national regulatory and supervisory authorities are intensifying their monitoring of criminals using the banking system with respect to their illegal and criminal income. As criminals attempt to hide their income, banks are most often among the financial institutions involved in "money laundering" and the transfer of criminal and illegal income across international borders. It happens because of the wide range of financial transactions that banks are engaged in. The speed of money transfers is almost instantaneous, and banks typically provide confidentiality due to legal requirements.

Money laundering and terrorism financing is being facilitated by numerous financial transactions and transformation of certain assets into others. Although the financial processes themselves are not illegal, they cannot be used by criminals to launder money. The most common tools of money laundering and terrorist financing by criminals are export-import, investment, lending, conversion operations and operations with securities. By means of these operations, the following purposes are achieved: concealment of criminal income sources, the creation of visibility of income legality; concealment

128 Deposit Guarantee Fund. (2015, February 16). ABOUT US. Retrieved from Deposit Guarantee Fund: http://www.fg.gov.ua/en/.

of persons who received criminal incomes and the provision of convenient and operative access to illegally obtained funds.

Simultaneously, it should be noted that besides providing services to the criminal bank client through which one implements money laundering or financing terrorism (which is an *external threat*), the bank can directly participate in money laundering, obtaining the economic effect of the provided services which will be considered as an *internal threat* of its activity.

Moreover, every year the mechanism of money laundering by criminals becomes more complicated, diversified and more "innovative". Criminals focus on countries with the least regulated banking system and take advantage of the imperfections in their regulation and supervision. Based on the aforementioned, relevance of money laundering and financing terrorism, as well as its complexity, there is a necessity for each state to build an effective financial monitoring system.[129]

Due to the fact that not only there is a money laundering problem in the banking system, but also the problem of terrorism financing, it has become more important for Ukraine over the past two years. Therefore, research of the process of financial monitoring system formation and its current status is extremely important.

Exploring the financial monitoring process of the Ukrainian banks, it should be noted that it was conforming with, and being influenced by, the numerous requirements of international organizations. These include the following:

- Financial Action Task Force on Money Laundering (FATF),
- Committee of Experts on the Evaluation of Anti-Money Laundering Measures and the Financing of Terrorism (MONEYVAL),
- The United Nations Office on Drugs and Crime (UNODC),
- The International Monetary Fund (IMF),
- The World Bank.

When analyzing the history and evolution of bank financial monitoring systems in Ukraine, it should be noted that the first initiatives date back to 1997, with Ukraine signing the Strasbourg's *Convention on Laundering, Search, Seizure and Confiscation of the Proceeds from Crime.*[130] This obligated the National Bank of Ukraine (NBU) to conform Ukrainian legislation to the Convention and to promulgate new regulations and rules that are necessary

129 Berezhnoy O. (2010) Assessment and management of risk using the services for legalization of criminal income or terrorist financing in the commercial bank: monograph / [S. O. Dmitrov, O. V. Merenkova, T. A. Medvid, M. O. Vaschenko]. – Sumy: "Ukrainian Academy of banking of the NBU". – 114 p.

130 Convention on laundering, search, seizure and confiscation of the proceeds: Convention from 17.12.97. – Access mode: http://zakon4.rada.gov.ua/laws/show/995_029.

to ensure the ability of public authorities to confiscate the income or property acquired through criminal activity. Simultaneously, the principles of the Convention obligated NBU to identify certain transactions in the banking sector as criminal and actively cooperate with foreign central banks and financial institutions to identify transactions involved in money laundering.

The first substantive national legislation (which touched on the financial monitoring and regulating of certain aspects of this process) was the Law of Ukraine "On banks and banking activity" dated 07.12.2000 # 2121-III.[131] It provides:

- procedure for the disclosure by banks of all necessary information (bank confidentiality) about the entities that are subjected to the requirement of compulsory financial monitoring;
- mechanism of development and implementation of internal financial monitoring rules of banks;
- term of banking verification by the NBU regarding their compliance with the legislation regulating relations in the sphere of combating money laundering.

The next step of conforming Ukrainian banking law to international standards for monitoring money laundering was a legislative consolidation of certain basic principles in August 2001, August, defined as "The Forty recommendations of the FATF". Thus, the joint Resolution of the Cabinet of Ministers of Ukraine and the National Bank of Ukraine "On Forty recommendations of the Financial Action Task Force (FATF)", # 1124 dated 28.08.01 was passed.[132]

However, despite the progress in reforming the regulatory framework for ensuring financial monitoring of banking activities, qualitative changes did not happen in this sphere in Ukraine. Further legal rules and regulations that would enhance the monitoring of and facilitating the identification of money laundering and financial monitoring procedures were not accepted. Numerous changes in the organizational structure of the NBU were technical and did not lead to a real decrease in the exposure volume of money laundering done through banks. In addition, there was also no progress in the adoption of "The Forty recommendations of the FATF". As a result, in 2001 Ukraine was included into the "black list" of FATF. This event caused numerous economic and financial sanctions against Ukraine.

131 On banks and banking activity: Law of Ukraine from 07.12.2000 # 2121-III. – Access mode: http://zakon3.rada.gov.ua/laws/show/2121-14.

132 On Forty recommendations of the Group from development of financial measures of fight against money laundering (FATF): Joint resolution of the Cabinet of Ministers of Ukraine and the National Bank of Ukraine from 28.08.01 # 1124. – Access mode: http://zakon5.rada.gov.ua/laws/show/1124-2001-%D0%BF.

Attempting to be removed from the "black list" by the FATF, the Resolution of NBU Board in 30.04.2002 "On approval of Methodological recommendations on the development of Ukraine's banks' programs with the aim of combating the legalization (laundering) of money obtained through criminal activities" #164 (repealed with 10.11.2011) was adopted.[133] The essence of the development programs was the involvement of all employees, regardless of their position, within their competence, to identify transactions with monetary funds or other property, related to laundering of money obtained through criminal means.

The pressure from international organizations led to the adoption of the law # 249-IV "On prevention and counteraction of legalization (laundering) of money obtained by criminal means" dated 28.11.2002 (no longer valid since 06.02.2015).[134] The law defined the required financial monitoring by banking regulators, their rights and obligations, as well as the sphere of their influence. The subject of financial monitoring was divided into two levels: primary and state. The action of the law has extended not only to citizens of Ukraine and the domestic economic entities, but also to foreigners and stateless people, foreign companies and their separate subdivisions.

At the same time, in accordance with the provisions of the law, the NBU was charged with the main duties regarding the financial monitoring of banks:

- supervision over the performing of requirements of the legislation by banks in the sphere of combating the legalization of funds obtained by illegal means and financing of terrorism;
- adoption of measures in case of non-compliance with legislation by banks;
- audit of professional training of the bank staff that is responsible for conducting internal financial monitoring.

The system of financial monitoring in Ukraine itself was divided into two levels: primary and state. The following are the primary financial monitoring subjects:

- banks, insurers (reinsurers), credit unions, pawnshops and other financial institutions;
- payment service organizations, members of payment systems, acquiring and clearing institutions;
- commodity, stock, and other exchanges;

133 On approval of methodological recommendations on the development of banks of Ukraine programs with the aim of combating the legalization (laundering) of money obtained by criminal means: Resolution of the NBU from 30.04.02 # 164. – Access mode: http://zakon3.rada.gov.ua/laws/show/v0164500-02.

134 On prevention and counteraction to legalization (laundering) of income obtained by criminal means: Law of Ukraine from 28.11.02 N° 249-IV. – Access mode: http://zakon5.rada.gov.ua/laws/show/249-15.

- professional participants of securities market;
- asset management companies;
- postal service operators and other institutions that conduct financial transactions from transfer funds;
- branches or representative offices of foreign business entities which provide financial services on the territory of Ukraine;
- business entities who provide intermediary services during transactions of sale and purchase of real estate;
- economic entities who carry out cash trading of precious metals, precious stones and products made of them, if the amount of financial transaction equals or exceeds UAH 150 thousand or the equivalent in foreign currency;
- economic entities who conduct lotteries and gambling including casino, electronic (virtual) casinos;
- notaries, lawyers, auditors, audit firms, individuals – entrepreneurs who provide accounting services, economic entities who provide legal services (except persons providing services within labor law relations);
- individuals – entrepreneurs and legal entities, which conduct cash financial transactions with goods (execute works, provide services), if the amount of such financial transaction equals or exceeds UAH 150 thousand, or the equivalent in foreign currency.

The following entities are performing state financial monitoring:

- National Bank of Ukraine;
- Ministry of Finance of Ukraine;
- Ministry of Justice of Ukraine;
- Ministry of Infrastructure of Ukraine;
- Ministry of Economic Development and Trade of Ukraine;
- Securities and Stock Market State Commission;
- State Commission for Regulation of Financial Services Markets of Ukraine;
- State service for financial monitoring of Ukraine.

The adoption of the Law "On prevention and counteraction to legalization (laundering) of money obtained by criminal means" has affected the organizational structure of the NBU. In February of 2003, an independent structural division of the Head office of the National Bank was established, referred to as the office of methodological, normative and organizational ensuring of financial monitoring.

Therefore, the adoption of this law can be considered the starting point for the establishment of a new financial monitoring system in Ukraine and the official delegation of the respective functions in the banking sector to NBU.

Along with NBU, the central executive authority plays a significant role in the state financial monitoring in Ukraine. The Central Executive authority implements state policy in the sphere of prevention and counteraction to money laundering, terrorist financing and financing of proliferation of weapons of mass destruction (at first this authority was called the State Department for financial monitoring, then from 28 September 2004 it was called the State Committee for financial monitoring of Ukraine, and from April 13, 2011–the State service for financial monitoring). This authority needs to collect all information on the use of financial intermediaries for the purpose of money laundering and the financing of terrorism, as well as to lead and coordinate the work of all state bodies of regulatory oversight and control in this field throughout Ukraine.

All the aforementioned changes in the national system of financial monitoring have led to the necessity of adopting additional rules, namely the Order of the State Financial Monitoring Department # 40 dated 24.04.2003 "On approval of requirements to organizing of financial monitoring by entities of initial financial monitoring in the sphere of prevention and counteraction to introduction into the legal treatment of income obtained by criminal means and terrorism financing".[135] This Order regulated the issues of internal financial monitoring. Thus, it determined the general requirements with respect to:

- assign the employee responsible for conducting financial monitoring, his rights, and duties;
- establish financial monitoring and conducting programs for its implementation;
- identify financial transactions that are subject to financial monitoring and which can be identified with the financing of terrorism;
- identify the position responsible for the monitoring of the relevant financial transactions, store relevant documents;
- develop procedures for the registration of entities engaged in certain types of financial transactions which are subject to financial monitoring;
- order the termination of relevant financial transactions;
- provide information regarding financial transactions that are subject to financial monitoring;
- train staff to identify financial transactions subjected to financial monitoring.

This order provided the framework for the internal financial monitoring of all entities of the first level, including banks. However, the specific mechanism for the internal financial monitoring of all entities of the first level was formed independently. The order determined only the necessary conditions for its organization and operation.

135 On approval of requirements on organization of financial monitoring by entities of initial financial monitoring: The order of the State Department of financial monitoring from 24.04.2003 # 40. – Access mode: http://zakon5.rada.gov.ua/laws/show/z0337-03.

Directly, the development of the regulatory framework for financial monitoring of banks took place by regulations and rules promulgated at the level of the Board of NBU and the orders of its departments. Thus, on 14.05.2003, Resolution of the Board of the National Bank of Ukraine "On approval of the Regulations on the implementation of financial monitoring by banks" # 189, was approved.[136] This Resolution regulated the following issues:

- identification and registration by banks of financial transactions subjected to financial monitoring, as well as their suspension and resumption;
- identification and classification of clients, based on the bank's risk criteria;
- providing information by banks to the State Service of Financial Monitoring in Ukraine on issues of combating money laundering and financing of terrorism;
- risk management of money laundering and financing of terrorism;
- personnel issues regarding bank employees responsible for internal financial monitoring.

The necessity of tracking and monitoring the implementation of NBU Regulations provisions led to the establishment of the Department for prevention of using banking system for money laundering and terrorism financing. It was formed on the basis of the existing Department of methodological, normative and organizational ensuring of financial monitoring in March 2005. The new department, as well as the previous one, remained a structural division of the head office of the National Bank of Ukraine, but it was responsible for considerably more tasks in the sphere of financial monitoring and, consequently, it had a wider range of powers.

The main tasks of the Department were:

- implementation of the regulatory and supervisory functions over banking activity in the sphere of prevention and counteraction of money laundering and financing of terrorism;
- development of the methodology for banks implementing the financial monitoring tasks;
- cooperation with banking supervisory authorities of other countries in the sphere of money laundering and terrorism financing.

According to assigned tasks, the Department performs the following functions:

- coordination of work of the NBU structural departments (in particular, at the regional level) regarding supervision over the implementation by banks

136 On approval of the regulation on the implementation by banks of financial monitoring: Resolution of the NBU from 14.05.03 # 189. – Access mode: http://zakon5.rada.gov.ua/laws/show/z0381-03.

of Ukraine's legislation on preventing money laundering and terrorism financing;
- development of norms and legal acts on prevention and counteraction of money laundering and terrorism financing;
- explanation to banks about the specific application of Ukraine's legislation norms and regulatory legal acts of the NBU in the sphere of combating money laundering and terrorism financing;
- providing methodological assistance by the National Bank of Ukraine to the territorial departments regarding exercising supervisory functions over banks';
- supervision over meeting the requirements of the Ukrainian legislation on prevention the legalization by banks;
- evaluation of statistical reporting data received from the territorial administrations of the National Bank of Ukraine regarding financial transactions that are subject to financial monitoring, the number of clients who are subject to identification, etc.[137]

The Department was guided by the Constitution of Ukraine, and all the aforementioned normative legal acts regarding financial monitoring, as well as recommendations of international organizations aimed at counteraction of money laundering and terrorism financing.

Based on the fact that, the Ukrainian normative base on issues of financial monitoring has been formed on the basis of international requirements, practical aspects of the provisions' implementation of the newly created legislation took into account the main principles of banking supervision of foreign organizations.

According to the Basel principles, the system of financial monitoring should:
- be based on standard approach or the risk assessment approach;
- provide documentary and field checks.

The standard approach assumes the same direct field supervision of all banks in the country by the same procedure within 1–3 years. Some differences in supervisory procedures may relate to banks of different size, specialization and geographic location. This approach is simple, but costly and time consuming in the long run. The results obtained in the framework of the standard financial monitoring are not operational and do not allow to quickly respond to situations or transactions involving money laundering or terrorism financing.

137 Kovalenko V. V. (2007) International experience in the sphere of prevention and counteraction to laundering of income obtained by criminal means and financing of terrorism: a monograph / V. V. Kovalenko, S. O. Dmitrov, A. V. Yezhov. – Суми: The Ukrainian Academy of banking of the NBU. – 112 p.

In turn, the monitoring based on the assessment of existing risks is aimed at the diversification of the testing procedures depending on the level of risk associated with possible money laundering or terrorism financing characteristic to a particular bank. The supervision based on risk assessment is aimed at the identification of the most significant risks characteristic of banks and further verification by the NBU during its examination with respect to how the bank manages these risks and how it is able to neutralize them. This considerably saves time, material and financial resources to check, and also substantially increases its effectiveness.

The only problem with financial monitoring based on risk assessment implementation is its methodology of conduct. Each international organization recommends to each central bank to develop it independently. In order to fully implement the concept of financial monitoring based on risk assessment, the Resolution of the Board of the National Bank of Ukraine "Methodology of risk assessment of violation of legislation requirements on financial monitoring by banks" # 458, was adopted on October 12, 2010. The Department of Financial Monitoring of the NBU for analysis and on-site supervision on combating money laundering and terrorism financing based its activity is covered by this Resolution.[138]

The aforementioned methodology is implemented in 3 stages.

1. Defining of relevant performance indicators of banking activities, within the possibilities of their application for the purpose of preventing money laundering or terrorism financing.
2. The formation of binary tables characteristics of acceptable risk values. In case of compliance of values with acceptable limits, we assign 0, otherwise–1.
3. Determining of the risk of banks to be used for the purpose of preventing money laundering terrorism financing on the basis of Bayesian analysis.

The distinctive feature of the suggested methodology of bank's activity analysis is economic transparency, that is the validity of economic reasons for assigning one or another risk assessment of using banks for money laundering or terrorism financing. This is achieved by specific types of information, based on which the probability of the risks of using banks for legalization of criminal proceeds or terrorism financing is evaluated.

138 Berezhnoy O. (2014) The definition of risk of the banking institutions according the using of its services for the legalization of criminal income or financing of terrorism during the inspection (): monograph / [Dmitrov S., Medvid T., Levchenko L., Butkovskaya T., Kuzmenko O. and others]. – Sumy: "Ukrainian Academy of banking of the NBU". – 103 p.

In particular, the following forms of statistical reporting of banks are used to determine the basic indicative indicators to assess the financial monitoring risk:

- form # 10 "Turnover balance sheet of bank";
- form # 200 "Report on cooperation of banks with specially authorized body on financial monitoring";
- form # 201 "Report on the number of individual types of customers who own bank accounts";
- form # 401 "Data about transactions carried out by means of payment cards issued to bank customers";
- form # 538 "Information about buying foreign currency on behalf of bank customers, other banks and authorized banks";
- form # 527 "Report on the turnover of cash foreign currency";
- form # 748 "Report on cash turnover of bank";
- form # 552 "Report on inflow from non-residents and selling of foreign currency".

Twenty-five basic indicative parameters are calculated based on the data of these reports. The indicators are calculated for the chosen period of time.

Furthermore, the calculation of risk on financial monitoring assumes the express assessment and probabilistic assessment. Probabilistic risk assessment on financial monitoring is conducted on the basis of the express assessment results.

Express risk assessment is based on the calculation of binary parameters (B). For this purpose, the estimate of limit (threshold) values is conducted for the identified characteristics (formation of interval of acceptable (critical) values). The state of each bank is characterized by a set of binary indicators (B) that take the values "1/"0" ("0" – in case of finding corresponding features in the allowed range of values, and "1" otherwise).

After identifying the empirical standards, each bank will be characterized by a set of binary indicators $B=\left(B_1,B_2,\ldots,B_n\right), n=25$. To determine the levels of risk on financial monitoring firstly the value $b_k$ – is the probability of the event $B_k=0$ and $g_k$ – is the probability of event $B_k=1$ for each bank of a certain group on all indicators $k=1\div n, n=25$ are calculated by the following formulas:

$$g_k=\frac{\sum_k B_k}{n},$$

$$b_k=1-g_k,$$

where $b_k$ – probability of the event $B_k = 0$, i.e., receiving characteristics of banking services on a value of binary indicator which is equal to zero in terms of k-the indicator.

$g_k$ – is the probability of an event $B_k = 1$, i.e., receiving characteristics of banking services on a value of binary indicator which is equal to one in terms of k-the indicator

After determining $b_k$ – the probability of the event $B_k = 0$, and $g_k$ – the probability of the event $B_k = 1$ parameters $\lambda_k$ and $\lambda_0$ are calculated by all indicators for each bank of a certain group by the following formulas:

$$\lambda_k = \ln\left(\frac{b_k(1-g_k)}{g_k(1-b_k)}\right), k = 1,\ldots,n \quad ,$$

$$\lambda_k = \ln\left(\frac{p(H2)}{p(H1)}\right) + \sum_{k=1}^{n} \ln\left(\frac{1-b_k}{1-g_k}\right).$$

p(H1) and p(H2) will be equal to 0.5, thus the following formula should be used to calculate $\lambda_0$:

$$\lambda_0 = \sum_{k=1}^{n} \ln\left(\frac{1-b_k}{1-g_k}\right).$$

After this $L$– the weighted sum of the binary indicators $b_k$ is determined by the formula:

$$L = \sum_{k=1}^{n} \lambda_k b_k.$$

Then according to the following formula, the integrated index of risk of violation of legislation requirements on financial monitoring by banks is calculated by the general formula:

$$p_B(H1) = \frac{1}{1 + e^{\{\lambda_0 + L\}}},$$

where $p_B(H1)$ is a composite indicator of risk of legislation requirements on financial monitoring violation by banks.

The level of risk for each bank is defined based on the obtained probabilistic risk assessment of using banks for laundering criminal income ($p_B(H1)$):

- if $0 \leq p_B(H1) < 0,3$, it is the normal level of risk;
- if $0,3 \leq p_B(H1) < 0,5$ it is an increased level of risk;
- if $0,5 \leq p_B(H1) < 0,7$, it is a high level of risk;
- if $0,7 \leq p_B(H1) \leq 1$, it is a critical level of risk.[139]

The developed methodology fully corresponds with international requirements to development of approach based on risk assessment in the sphere of financial monitoring, and ensures highly effective supervision aimed at identification of existing and potential threats in banks. It allows to solve problems of financial monitoring in the banking system of Ukraine.

Nevertheless, this methodology has some drawbacks. The results of the risk level do not provide the ability to determine what exactly influenced its occurrence. That is, within a subsequent on-site inspection it is required to carry out the complex analysis of the bank's activities. This problem was solved by practices of the NBU and researchers within the development of the factor analysis methodology of the risk of money laundering and terrorism financing (in particular, the results of the developments are presented in monographs[140]). However, they did not find the practical implementation of similar regulations of Board of the NBU. This is due to the rotation of leadership of some departments of the NBU and significant bureaucratic procedures regarding the adoption of any legal regulation or rule in Ukraine.

The next significant step within the improvement of the national system of financial monitoring in Ukraine was the adoption of the resolution of the Cabinet of Ministers of Ukraine dated 10.12.2003 (repealed with 29.05.2015) "On the Unified State Informational System in the sphere of prevention and counteraction to legalization (laundering) of incomes obtained by criminal means and terrorism financing" # 1896.[141] The peculiarity and importance of this legal act was the combination of information databases of the state bodies that within their competence carry out activities in the sphere of combating

139 Dmitrov S. The practical application of Bayesian analysis in the implementation of financial monitoring in banks (2011): monograph / [O. V. Kuzmenko, T. A. Medvid, L. G. Levchenko and others]. – Sumy "Ukrainian Academy of banking of the NBU", 2011. – 46 p.

140 National risk assessment of legalization of funds obtained by criminal means, financing of terrorism and proliferation of weapons of mass destruction: new challenges/ Dmitrov S. O., Medvid T. A., Kuzmenko O. V., Boyko A. O. – Cherkassy: publisher Chabanenko Y. A., 2015. – 270 p.

141 On the Unified state information system in the sphere of prevention and counteraction to legalization (laundering) of income obtained by criminal means and financing of terrorism: Resolution of the Cabinet of Ministers of Ukraine from 10.12.2003 # 1896. – Access mode: http://zakon3.rada.gov.ua/laws/show/1896-2003-%D0%BF.

money laundering and terrorism financing. This gave the opportunity to provide for the sharing of information between all state authorities and to conduct a comprehensive analysis of information on money laundering. Subsequently, the informational databases of such state authorities were joint: State Service for Financial Monitoring, State Customs Service (nowadays the Customs of the State Fiscal Service), State Tax Administration (currently the State Fiscal Service), Ministry of Internal Affairs, State Border Service, State Committee of Statistics, State Commission on Securities and Stock Market (currently, National Commission on Securities and Stock Market), State Commission for Regulation of Financial Services Markets of Ukraine (nowadays the State Commission for Regulation of Financial Services Markets), the NBU, Security Service of Ukraine, the Ministry of Justice, the Ministry of Economy (currently Ministry of Economic Development and Trade), the Ministry of Finance, the Control and Audit Service of Ukraine (currently the State Audit Service of Ukraine), State Property Fund, State Service of Communications (currently the State Service of Special Communication Administration and Information Protection of Ukraine), State Committee for Land Resources currently the State Service of Ukraine on Geodesy, Cartography and Cadastre).

In order to replace the aforementioned provisions, the Resolution of the Cabinet of Ministers of Ukraine from 14.05.2015 # 299 “Certain issues of the Unified State Informational System in the sphere of prevention and counteraction to legalization (laundering) of criminal incomes, terrorism financing and financing of proliferation of weapons of mass destruction”, was adopted. The Resolution regulates the procedure for determining national informational resources and the procedure for providing access to them to ensure the functioning of this Unified State Informational System, as well as the principles of its functioning and development.[142] On the basis of this Resolution, in addition to previous subjects of Unified State Informational System, the Treasury and the Prosecutor General’s Office of Ukraine were added, and the Ministry of Finance, State Service of Special Communication Administration and Information Protection of Ukraine, State Service of Ukraine on Geodesy, Cartography and Cadastre, were excluded.

The continuation of international organizations’ influence on the process of transformation of the regulation of financial monitoring of banking activity in

142 Some issues of the Unified state information system in the sphere of prevention and counteraction to legalization (laundering) of income from crime, terrorist financing and financing of proliferation of weapons of mass destruction: Resolution of the Cabinet of Ministers of Ukraine from 14.05.2015 # 299. – Access mode: http://zakon3.rada.gov.ua/laws/show/299-2015-%Dc%BF.

Ukraine is evident in the effective measures of impact on the property of the offenders. Thus, on 21.04.2011, the Law of Ukraine # 3266-VI "On Amendments to Certain Legislative Acts on the Seizure of Assets Related to Terrorism Financing and Financial Transactions Suspended Pursuant to the Decisions Taken on the Basis of the UN Security Council Resolutions and Establishing a Procedure for the Access to Such Assets", was adopted.[143] This Law established a judicial procedure for seizure of assets related to terrorism financing and related financial operations and money laundering, as well as the involvement of the Security Service of Ukraine and the Ministry of Foreign Affairs of Ukraine in the process of access to these assets.

Numerous changes in the Ukrainian legislation (tax, administrative, criminal codes etc.) in particular, and the transformation of the international financial monitoring system in general, have led to the adoption of the new Law of Ukraine "On Prevention and Counteraction to Legalization (Laundering) of Proceeds from Crime, Terrorism Financing and the Financing of Proliferation of Weapons of Mass Destruction" # 1702-VII dated 14.10.2014.[144] Thus, the new law takes into account the agreements of Ukraine with the aim of obtaining the tranches from IMF and proposals of the experts of Group on development of financial measures of combating of money laundering and terrorism financing (FATF).

In addition, it also includes the risk of financing the proliferation of weapons of mass destruction. As a result, an integrated improvement of national legislation in the sphere of financial monitoring and cooperation mechanism with international organizations in combating money laundering took place. The main changes concerned the list of entities subject to initial financial monitoring and their functions, and the list of financial transactions subject to compulsory financial monitoring. In addition, the new Law included a detailed definition of actions that can be linked to money laundering. Insurance (reinsurance) brokers, distributors of state lotteries, law offices and associations, and business entities that provide services of accounting, have been included into the list of entities subject to initial monitoring.

143 On amendments to some legislative acts concerning the arrest of assets linked to the financing of terrorism and related financial transactions, stopped in accordance with the decision taken under resolutions of UN Security Council and determine the order of access to such assets: Law of Ukraine from 21.04.2011 # 3266-VI – Access mode: http://zakon3.rada.gov.ua/laws/show/3266-17.

144 On prevention and counteraction to legalization (laundering) of income from crime, terrorist financing and financing of proliferation of weapons of mass destruction: Law of Ukraine from 14.10.2014 # 1702-VII – Access mode: http://zakon5.rada.gov.ua/laws/show/1702-18.

In the framework of financial monitoring of banking activity, the changes have been related to identification and verification of a client. For example, to establish the ultimate beneficial owner, the bank was required to request the customer's information and/or documents confirming the presence of its ownership structure. In addition, the law specified the term "foreign bank branch", and also defined, for which offences banks and branches of foreign banks that are responsible.

A significant stage in the development of the financial monitoring system of banking activity in Ukraine was the adopted on 26.06.2015, the resolution of the NBU Board "On approval of the regulations on the implementation of financial monitoring by banks" # 417.[145] The importance of this legal act is explained in the accumulation of all aspects of financial monitoring in banking activity in Ukraine and their clear structuring. Thus, in the Resolution of the NBU Board are defined the following issues:

1. Requirements with respect to the bank's internal documents on financial monitoring.
2. The construction and operation of the risk management system for the prevention of money laundering and terrorism financing.
3. The order of sending notification requiring the registration/deregistration of the entity of initial financial monitoring.
4. The procedure of verifying a customer's identification.
5. The procedure of analysis, detection and registration of financial transactions.
6. The procedure of providing information to the specially authorized body (State Financial Monitoring Service of Ukraine).
7. The order to terminate or resume financial operations and to implement the decisions (orders) of the competent authority (State Financial Monitoring Service of Ukraine).
8. The procedure for approval of appointment and dismissal of the responsible employee of the bank.
9. Requirements to the rules of financial monitoring of the banking group.

The adopted document summarized all the previous achievements of the national system of financial monitoring of banking during the past fifteen years and has developed a complex set of requirements needed to be implemented by banks in Ukraine.

145 On approval of the regulation on the implementation by banks of financial monitoring: Resolution of the NBU from 26.06.2015 # 417. – Access mode: http://zakon5.rada.gov.ua/laws/show/v0417500-15.

In addition to the above, every year additional measures with respect to the plan of measures on anti-money laundering and combatting terrorism financing by the Cabinet of Ministers and the NBU is implemented. For instance, in 2015: the Cabinet of Ministers and the NBU have accepted the Resolution "On approving of plan of activities for 2015 on prevention and counteraction to legalization (laundering) of incomes from criminal activities, terrorism financing and financing of proliferation of mass destruction weapons" # 99[146]).

The plan typically contains activities regarding:

- coordination of activities of all state bodies in the sphere of combating money laundering, terrorism financing and financing the proliferation of weapons of mass destruction;
- further implementation of the provisions of international organizations into national legislation;
- necessity of adopting changes in the agreements and rules with combatting money laundering, terrorism financing and the financing of the proliferation of weapons of mass destruction;
- increase the efficiency of law-enforcement and other state bodies;
- professional development of specialists of state bodies of regulation, supervision and control;
- participation in international cooperation etc.

Moreover, in this document, state bodies responsible for the performance of mentioned actions are defined, as well as the timeframes for their implementation.

Completing the study of specific features of conducting of banking activity financial monitoring in Ukraine, it should be noted that certain aspects for the responsibility of entities of initial financial monitoring are defined in the administrative code of Ukraine.[147] For example, the following will entail imposition fines:

- violation of requirements for the identification, verification, study, and clarification of information about the client;
- failure to submit, untimely submission, violation of procedures for submission, or submission of false information related to analysis of financial

146 On approving plan of activities for 2015 of prevention and counteraction to legalization (laundering) of income from crime, terrorist financing and financing of proliferation of weapons of mass destruction: Resolution of the Cabinet of Ministers of Ukraine and the National Bank of Ukraine from 11.03.2015 # 99. – Access mode: http://zakon3.rada.gov.ua/laws/show/99-2015-%D0%BF.

147 The code of Ukraine about administrative violations dated from 07.12.1984 # 8073-X. – Access mode: http://zakon4.rada.gov.ua/laws/show/80731-10.

transactions, with respect to the financial monitoring by the State Financial Monitoring Service of Ukraine.

In turn, the Criminal Code of Ukraine[148] defines the level of responsibility of individuals who committed a crime, depending on the amount of illegal income, the number of times the individual has been prosecuted for such actions, and the number of criminal groups.

In summary, it is fair to highlight the following key points.

First, the presence of the significant number of statutory acts, and the number of individuals and agencies regulating the process of financial monitoring of banking activity in Ukraine (about twenty), do not allow the rules to be implemented effectively. In addition, the provisions defined in the laws and regulations are implemented improperly by the entities of initial financial monitoring improperly. Entities are not familiar (to sufficient extent) with a significant number of these provisions. It requires the regulation of even more activities in order to increase awareness of the banks with legal requirements.

Second, given that the current strategy of reform of the regional structure of the NBU is to reduce territorial divisions, the problem of on-site financial monitoring of Ukrainian banks becomes paramount. Not only must the methodology for risk assessment of violation by banks of requirements of legislation on financial monitoring be improved, but also the effective control over the accuracy of the statistics, which is submitted to the NBU, must be improved as well. The off-site control will be adequate only if the correct information is submitted.

Third, there are still significant challenges for the prosecution of criminals, not only for the system of financial monitoring of banking activity in Ukraine, but also for the entire system of combating financial, administrative and criminal offences. Just revealing the bad behavior does not mean that the court will find the person guilty and that he will get a fair punishment. Moreover, the problem of judicial corruption in Ukraine is very high, hence even the most effective legislation in the sphere of financial monitoring of banking activity and appropriate actions of the NBU in identifying individuals and banks which are engaged in money laundering or financing of terrorism, will not eliminate this problem without a fair trial.

148 The criminal code of Ukraine from 05.04.2001 // Gazette of Verkhovna Rada of Ukraine. – 2001. No 25–26, art 131; with subsequent amendments and additions.

## 5 The Likely Economic Impacts of New Banking Regulation in Ukraine

During 2014–2015, Ukrainian economy was in deep crisis primarily due to the internal problems of the country, which have accumulated over the last years. Among main reasons include a decrease in demand for products produced by Ukrainian companies; a rapid devaluation of the national currency; bankruptcies of numerous banks; and the ineffective decisions of the executive authority as well as military operations in the East of the country.

Regulation of the banking system is of paramount importance in the process of economic recovery of Ukraine. Due to the fact that currently Ukraine has a bank-oriented model of the financial market, the accumulation of financial resources and their reallocation takes place through banks. Thus, the new approach of banking regulation will play a significant role in the recovery of Ukrainian economy.

Considering the main problems of the banking system of Ukraine, the actions of the regulator in the present conditions and future periods should be directed to the following:

- reduction in the circulation of money in national and foreign currency through the banking system and the shadow sector;
- decrease in the deposit and loan portfolios of banks;
- increased use of bank operations for anti-money laundering with related parties;
- increase quick and transparent procedures for mergers and acquisitions of banks;
- increase the investment attractiveness of Ukraine's banking sector by simplifying the process of the withdrawal dividends in foreign currency by investors;
- improve the public and entrepreneurs' confidence in the banking system of Ukraine and the effectiveness of the NBU.

First of all, it should be noted that the major problem of the financial system of Ukraine is inconsistency between state interests, individuals, and legal entities. Inefficiency of the numerous banking reforms and processes, as well as development of the shadow economy, is caused by the absence of dialogue between the mentioned-above parties. The banking sector has significant challenges with domestic currency fluctuations and foreign currency reserves due to the growth of the shadow banking market, triggered by the establishment of the administrative currency exchange restrictions by the NBU, imposed by the crisis events in 2014–2015. Restrictions were aimed at stabilizing the domestic currency and the foreign exchange markets, but it had an opposite effect.

This situation caused problems for private businesses. When a Ukrainian company purchases foreign currency through a bank, NBU almost always examines the contract with a foreign supplier, obliging the companies to convert the profit obtained in foreign currency into hryvnias. Moreover, conversion of the domestic currency into the foreign one was not done at the market rate, but at an arbitrary rate set by the central bank, which was significantly different from the real market rate. There are numerous cases, when the NBU demanded to revise the contracts, which led to confusion with foreign partners as well as the delayed delivery of goods and services. Thus, the Central Bank was forced to find alternative ways of conducting business.

During last period, in Ukraine reappeared currency exchange (FX) kiosks for serving financial companies for several months. The confirmation of this was the sharp rise of general licenses for foreign exchange transactions in 2016 issued by the NBU. Accordingly, there was 28 private exchange points in 2016 that is 24 more than the previous year. This indicates that the exchange rates of the banking sector go into the "shadow". Thus, all gains for the return of domestic and foreign currency from the shadow banking market to the banking sector in 2004–2008 were lost.

In order to address mentioned-above issues, the NBU Board approved Resolution # 342 "On resolving the situation in the money and foreign exchange markets of Ukraine"[149] from 07.06.2016. According to this resolution, the maximum amount of foreign currency in cash and bank metals increased from 6 thousand UAH to 12 thousand UAH in the equivalent. Moreover, restrictions on the amount of selling bank metals transaction will not apply to coins made from precious metals (including investment coins of Ukraine). NBU also eased the requirement for mandatory sale proceeds in Ukraine of foreign currency by legal entities from 75% to 65%. Unfortunately, these actions by the NBU were not timely, having no impact on those businesses, which have already carried out their operations in the shadow sector.

Also, the restrictions introduced in 2014–2015 had a negative effect on the general public, which was not able to exchange money at any time and for the desired volume. It led to a decrease of the number of foreign exchange transactions through the banks. It can be explained by the lack of the foreign currency in the banks as well as low exchange rates. Meanwhile, "the black market" met the needs of the general population without any restrictions. The Resolution of the Board of the NBU # 341 "On amendments to some legislative

149 On resolving the situation in the money and foreign exchange markets of Ukraine: Resolution of the NBU from 07.06.2016 # 342. – Access mode: http://zakon3.rada.gov.ua/laws/show/v0342500-16.

acts of the National Bank of Ukraine" from 07.06.2016[150] was adopted in order to redirect foreign exchange transactions back to the banking system. It set out which foreign currencies can be converted by the banks and financial institutions. Furthermore, the National Bank has also simplified the paperwork required for foreign exchange transactions. Nevertheless, each individual who desires to buy foreign currency is required to present a identification documents and proof of current residency. All these restrictions and their subsequent partial liberalization had a negative impact on the reputation of the banking sector in Ukraine among the general population and entrepreneurs, and once again confirmed the untimely regulatory actions by NBU.

Requirements of the internal bank activities in Ukraine have also undergone permanent transformations and innovations. Banks and financial institutions that exchange currency can change the exchange rates of buying and selling foreign currencies during the operational (working) day. This allowed a bank to reduce risks that may arise because of the changes in market conditions, and reduce the spread between the buying and selling rates of foreign exchange. Also, different foreign exchange rates can be set at cash desks, banks, financial institutions, their subdivisions and currency exchanges in different locations. This allows banks and financial institutions to respond better to regional variations in the currency markets. At the same time, the implementation of cash transactions conversion of one foreign currency into another allowed banks to use their own commercial rate, rather than the official rate of the National Bank.[151]

Unfortunately, in 2016 the foreign currency exchange risk is very high due to the fluctuations in the rate of foreign currencies with the value of the UAH, as well as the restructuring program and the conversion of foreign currency loans. Existing problems are mainly associated with overly strict administrative measures of currency regulation and therefore this situation will create additional difficulties for banks. The NBU cannot completely abandon these measures due to risk of future economic and financial crises, as confidence in the public sector is lost.

A significant problem for Ukrainian banks is the amount of deposit and loan portfolios. Nowadays, the volume of deposits is gradually increasing, while the amount of loans is decreasing due to high interest rates. Thus, Ukrainian

---

150 On amendments to some legislative acts of the National Bank of Ukraine: Resolution of the NBU from 07.06.2016 # 341. – Access mode: http://zakon4.rada.gov.ua/laws/show/v0341500-16.

151 The National Bank of Ukraine continues to temper currency regulation: Press-Centre of NBU from 08.06.2016 – Access mode: http://www.bank.gov.ua/control/uk/publish/article?art_id=32236335.

banks have an excess of liquidity. The banking system benefits the private sector to a lesser degree than it potentially could. Due to decreased loan volume, banks are likely not to lend according to prudential banking requirements and standards, which might lead to an increased amount of the non-performing loans. Thus, it requires more attention from the NBU, as the crisis of 2008–2009 showed the importance of carefully assessing and monitoring borrowers.

The decrease of the performance indicators of the banks in 2016 can be explained by the existing macroeconomic conditions and the state of the banking market. A key criterion is lending by the banking sector. Analysis found that in the banking sector this indicator fell in 2016. Accordingly, it showed a negative impact on the economy.

A major challenge for the banking system of Ukraine is accelerating the pace of the increase in minimum capital. Banking institutions were required to increase capital to 500 million UAH to 11 January 2017, whereas before they had time to 2020. On the one hand, it will improve their financial stability and increase capacity for risks resistance. In addition, the capital increase should increase lending to the economy, which is one of the factors accelerating an economic growth. But on the other hand, it can lead to an artificial reduction in business activity in the sector. The disappearance of small banks from the market may not only not improve stability, but may lead to bank monopolies controlling the banking sector.

However, to maintain its position in the market, a bank can use alternative scenarios of capitalization. The National Anti-Corruption Bureau considered five options to increase the authorized capital of 500 million UAH:

- available cash;
- simplified / accelerated liquidation of the bank;
- search for equity investors / search for subordinated debt;
- association with one or more other market players / acquisitions;
- granting limited licenses.

Overall, the NBU has tried to clean up and consolidate the private banking sector. Banks have had to find a market niche for operating or abandon the market at the present time. Given the current investment climate, a massive replenishment of statutory capital is unlikely to happen.

At the same time, these measures can be seen as incentives for mergers and acquisitions in the banking sector. Currently, drafts of laws regarding the simplification of the procedures, such as winding up of the bank as well as mergers and acquisition, are under the process of adoption. However, these reforms can only encourage the merger of existing banks and minimize red tape.

Recently, one of the major problems is the ban on the withdrawal of foreign investor's dividends in a foreign currency. Numerous investors are unwilling to invest in Ukrainian entities because of these restrictions. In this regard, the investment potential of Ukraine is reduced, subsequently, direct foreign investments are not increasing as occurred in past years. The main investors are Cyprus and the Netherlands, where the wealth of Ukrainian oligarchs is held.

In order to improve the investment climate, the NBU decided to allow the repatriation of dividends to foreign investors during 2014–2015.The Resolution of Cabinet of Minister of Ukraine # 342[152] provides that such dividends should be repatriated to issuers of corporate rights and shares for which dividends should be paid, or the depository institution should maintain a securities account of a foreign investor or return them directly to foreign investor. In order to repatriate dividends abroad, each individual can choose only one authorized bank. The procedure for changing the authorized bank serving those operations is similar to the procedure required for the import of goods.[153]

The National Bank of Ukraine sets the maximum amount of dividends, which are allowed to be repatriated. During the calendar month, a person can return abroad dividends only within the total amount. That amount may not exceed the greater of these limit values – $ 1 million USD (equivalent) or 10% of the total amount of dividends to be repatriated. If the amount subject to the 10% restriction is over 5 million USD (equivalent), the maximum amount of repatriation of dividends during the calendar month may not exceed $ 5 million USD (equivalent). Such restrictions were imposed because the amount of the repatriated dividends could have influenced the foreign currency exchange market.

This decision will satisfy foreign investors since they will be allowed to receive and transfer their dividends abroad. Moreover, the pressure, which currently exists on the interbank foreign currency exchange markets, will be relieved. The NBU was planning to allow foreigners to receive and transfer dividends from 2014–2016. Due to the introduced actions of the NBU, improvement of the investment potential in Ukraine is expected, which will lead to increased inflows of the foreign currencies in the country.[154]

---

152 On resolving the situation in the money and foreign exchange markets of Ukraine: Resolution of the NBU from 07.06.2016 # 342. – Access mode: http://zakon3.rada.gov.ua/laws/show/v0342500-16.

153 On resolving the situation in the money and foreign exchange markets of Ukraine: Resolution of the NBU from 07.06.2016 # 342. – Access mode: http://zakon3.rada.gov.ua/laws/show/v0342500-16.

154 The National Bank of Ukraine continues to temper currency regulation: Press-Centre of NBU from 08.06.2016. – Access mode: http://www.bank.gov.ua/control/uk/publish/article?art_id=32236335.

However, this may not be a positive trend. Sometimes foreign transactions can cause financial machinations of related entities, which will lead to significant losses into the economy of Ukraine. Furthermore, the Law of Ukraine # 218-VIII "On Amendments to Certain Legislative Acts of Ukraine regarding liability associated with the bank individuals" from 02.03.2015, was adopted.[155] As part of legislations changes, Deposit Guarantee Fund for individuals was given powers to deal with claims for compensation of damages caused by insolvent banks to related parties. At the beginning of July 2015, on the basis of principals issued by the Fund, there were 326 criminal lawsuits against thefts involved in failing banks for a total amount of 64 billion UAH.[156]

Also in 2016, the National Bank of Ukraine sent a large number of letters to banks, which required banks to disclose the direct and indirect owners of these financial institutions. Most of accusations were related to loans, which were made to enterprises, which were owned by the direct or indirect shareholders of the bank. The National Bank may require banks to list the related entities that are indirect owners of the bank. That's why the bank are obliged to set out in detail whether these related entities are doing business, or borrowing from, the bank. Thereafter the NBU can apply sanctions for violations of related party rules. Due to the active actions taken by the NBU in this area, the reduction of such crimes is expected.[157]

Additionally, the NBU should take actions to restore the public trust in the banking system. Uncertainty remains regarding the future of banking system, creates mutual distrust among banks, as well as raising skepticism related to the banks themselves from the households and non-bank institutions and enterprises. This helps explain the volume of withdrawals from their accounts, deposit withdrawals, especially in foreign currency. There are also problems with the cost of fundraising, including in the interbank market. It leads to the high cost of bank lending for the private sector and possibility that they will not return to the banks in the future to borrow.

The National Bank of Ukraine has revised the limits on the amount of cash withdrawals from the accounts of banks clients to improve the confidence of the general public in the banking sector. Customers of the bank are now

155 On Amendments to Certain Legislative Acts of Ukraine regarding liability associated with the bank individuals: Law of Ukraine from 02.03.2015. – Access mode: http://zakon4.rada.gov.ua/laws/show/218-19.

156 Golovina Y. S. (2015) Crisis regulation of Ukrainian banking system in the period 2014 – the first half of 2015: Global and national problems of the economy. – V. 7 – Access mode: http://global-national.in.ua/archive/7-2015/141.pdf.

157 On the approval of the resolution on definition of bank related persons from 12.05.2015 # 315: Resolution of NBU – Access mode: http://zakon3.rada.gov.ua/laws/show/v0315500-15.

allowed to withdraw cash in foreign currency and banking metals equal to 100 thousand UAH per day instead of 50 thousand UAH per day. The restrictions on the amount of cash withdrawals in local currency (which was equal to 500 thousand UAH per day) are also changed. This decision should contribute to the further restoring confidence in the banking system and strengthening the inflow of deposits both in local and foreign currencies.[158 159]

The new approaches to banking regulation by the National Bank of Ukraine have ambiguously influenced the Ukrainian economy. Furthermore, military actions in the East of the country and negative conjuncture changes in the real sector of the economy significantly affected the performance of these tools, which were introduced by the National Bank of Ukraine. However, each of the measures implemented by the National Bank of Ukraine had a considerable lag which minimized their effectiveness.

Significant number of issues was not resolved. For instance, there is still no solution on how to solve the problem of currency loans to individuals, returning deposits in foreign currencies, as well no rules on debt restructuring for corporate borrowers. Also, there are many open issues regarding the creditors rights' protection, which increases the effect of non-performing debt problems and the slowdowns of the normalization of process of financing of the banking institutions. Moreover, there is no transparent legal framework, which will define the obligations of the international bodies regarding the regulation of the banking sector in Ukraine. Thus, the new methods for regulating the banking system of Ukraine should not be measured quantitatively (how many instruments were used), but evaluated by qualitative criteria (adequacy of the impact and timeliness of the results).

## 6 Outlook

In 2016–2017, the banking system of Ukraine faced the problems that have accumulated during all of the years of independence. The imbalances in the banking system of Ukraine can be outlined not only by the consequences of the Global Financial Crises, but also, to a greater extent, by the internal

158 The National Bank of Ukraine continues to temper currency regulation: Press-Centre of NBU from 08.06.2016 – Access mode: http://www.bank.gov.ua/control/uk/publish/article?art_id=32236335.

159 On resolving the situation in the money and foreign exchange markets of Ukraine: Resolution of the NBU from 07.06.2016 # 342 – Access mode: http://zakon3.rada.gov.ua/laws/show/v0342500-16.

problems of the banking system, which are caused by the weak level of regulation of banks operating in Ukraine.

All banking sectors, whether they are state or private (including banks with foreign and Russian capital), carry out their activities in their own interests, and not necessarily in the interest of society, which in the end could harm the financial security of Ukraine. State banks are providing credit to state-owned enterprises, and the losses from the non-repayment of loans are covered by the recapitalization of their statutory funds from the state budget; that is by taxes paid by the general population and business entities in Ukraine.

Private banks in Ukraine, which are banks owned by 80% or more by oligarchs lend to their own enterprises at the expense of deposit resources (deposits of the population and medium-sized businesses) or withdraw funds from offshore zones.

Banks with foreign capital, although they carry out their activities without violating the laws of Ukraine, often lend to households and business entities at very high interest rates.

Separating the banks with Russian capital, we note that their activities in the context of a military conflict in the east of Ukraine, aimed at maintaining financial impact on the Ukrainian economy through the introduction of strategically important telecommunication, energy and fuel industries in the statutory capital.

In parallel, although the NBU is trying to close many of the weaker or insolvent banks, the closure of many banks is political in nature. At the same time, the activation of the Ukrainian credit market by reducing the discount rate did not lead to the revival of lending, as real interest rates in banks did not decrease and did not correspond to the real economic conditions in Ukraine and improve the possibilities of borrowers repaying these loans.

The main focus for the strategy of developing the system of regulation of the banking system of Ukraine should include the following provisions:

- implementation of European regulation and best practices of law not only in the field of banking supervision, but also in the entire financial sector of Ukraine, which will enable the solution for the complex problems of the credit and money markets of Ukraine;
- monitoring by the NBU the final implementation of the "Basel II" standards and the transition in 2019 to ensure compliance of the banking legislation of Ukraine with the provision of "Basel III", which will lead to the rapid integration of Ukraine's banking system into the global financial space;
- confirm by statute the degree of responsibility of the NBU for the determination and implementation of the tasks of monetary and credit policy and prudential supervision of banks;

- set out and develop the mechanisms for corporate social responsibility of both Ukrainian banks and the NBU, which should lead to increasing the responsibility of these structures to society;
- introduce effective, scientific and practically-based methodology for assessing money laundering risks and terrorist financing, which will reduce the use of Ukrainian banks in criminal schemes;
- improve the efficiency of the procedures for the liquidation of banks to eliminate abuses by the government and shareholders in the process;
- return to the strategy of a mega-regulator in the financial sector of Ukraine, and with the NBU to leave the functions of regulation of the monetary and credit system, which will ensure the stability of the monetary unit, the constancy and availability of the cost of borrowing and the impartiality of banking supervision;
- based on the national banking system specifics, formulate the mechanism for managing the reserves of Ukrainian banks, depending on their size and volumes of financial activity, which will increase the level of competition in the Ukrainian banking system at all levels;
- restore the positive image of the NBU and the banking system of Ukraine as a whole, in order to restore the confidence of the general population in the banking system.

It is fair to note that only the change of the regulatory system of Ukrainian banks and the activities of the NBU will create conditions for the internal development of the monetary and credit system, will ensure the formation of a favorable investment climate for the emergence of transnational European and world banks. It will ensure the direction of financial resources for the structural adjustment of the economy of Ukraine, which will be based on the development of innovative activities.

## 7 Conclusions

During 25 years of independence, the system of banking regulation and supervision in Ukraine has been transformed drastically. Ukraine had formed a strong regulatory framework and optimized system of the National Bank of Ukraine, which is currently functioning. During this economic and development period, the NBU has been attempting to implement leading international best practices of regulation and supervision of the banking system and adjusting it to the operating conditions of Ukrainian banks.

Nonetheless, the currently existing system of banking regulation and supervision in Ukraine is still in the development phase and cannot be considered as fully effective. The main problem of the Ukrainian system of banking regulation is practical implementation of the provisions established in the regulations and laws and the articles, which do not contradict each other. Banking regulation should not be populist by nature, and should comply with the current conditions of the financial and real sectors in the country's economy. The measures applied by the National Bank of Ukraine should have a long-term effect, and should not just react to urgent current problems in order to improve politicians' rating. Moreover, the financial resources allocated for reforming banking regulation in Ukraine and implementing new monitoring systems of the banks, should be controlled through accurate financial reporting and independent parties.

Thus, the European model of development, as determined by competent and unbiased regulators and officials, should be the basis of a transparent, impartial and effective regulatory and supervisory banking system. At the same time, European best practices of banking supervision should be adopted and adapted to the peculiarities of the Ukrainian banking system financing.

## 8 Bibliography

Aborchy O. V. (2013) Analysis of the evolution and the current state of the banking system of Ukraine. Strategy and mechanisms of regulation of industrial development. – P. 193–209. – Access mode: http://nbuv.gov.ua/UJRN/sim_2013_2013_17.

Association Agreement between the European Union and their member states, of the one part, and Ukraine, of the other part (European Union, 2014) – Access mode: https://eeas.europa.eu/sites/eeas/files/association_agreement_ukraine_2014_en.pdf.

Basel Committee – Core Principles Access mode: http://www.bis.org/list/bcbs/tid_25/index.htm.

Berezhnoy O. (2010) Assessment and management of risk using the services for legalization of criminal income or terrorist financing in the commercial bank: monograph / [S. O. Dmitrov, O. V. Merenkova, T. A. Medvid, M. O. Vaschenko]. – Sumy: "Ukrainian Academy of banking of the NBU". – 114 p.

Berezhnoy O. (2014) The definition of risk of the banking institutions according the using of its services for the legalization of criminal income or financing of terrorism during the inspection (): monograph / [Dmitrov S., Medvid T., Levchenko L., Butkovskaya T., Kuzmenko O. and others]. – Sumy: "Ukrainian Academy of banking of the NBU". – 103 p.

Borodkin A. (2015) (Sisetska A., Nikolenko O. (n.d.)) Ukraine. In the Banking Regulation Review (Vol. 6). London, United Kingdom: Gideon Roberton.

BTI (2016). Ukraine Country Report. Bertelsmann Stiftung's Transformation Index. Bertelsmann Stiftung.

Code of Ukraine on Administrative Offences (*Кодекс України про адміністративні правопорушення*) from 07.12.1984 # 8073-X – Access mode: http://zakon3.rada.gov.ua/laws/show/80731-10.

Convention on laundering, search, seizure and confiscation of the proceeds (*Конвенція про відмивання, пошук, арешт та конфіскацію доходів, одержаних злочинним шляхом*): Convention from 17.12.97. – Access mode: http://zakon4.rada.gov.ua/laws/show/995_029.

Credit activities: Resolution of the NBU from 28.09.1995 # 246 – Access mode: http://zakon2.rada.gov.ua/laws/show/v0246500-95.

Criminal Code of Ukraine: Resolution of the VRU from 05.04.2001 # 2341-III // Gazette of Verkhovna Rada of Ukraine. – 2001. № 25–26.

Deposit Guarantee Fund. (2105, February 16) – Access mode: http://www.fg.gov.ua/en/.

Dmitrov S. O. (Medvid T. A., Kuzmenko O. V., Boyko A. O.) National risk assessment of legalization of funds obtained by criminal means, financing of terrorism and proliferation of weapons of mass destruction: new challenges. – Cherkassy, 2015. – 270 p.

Dmitrov S. The practical application of Bayesian analysis in the implementation of financial monitoring in banks (2011): monograph / [O. V. Kuzmenko, T. A. Medvid, L. G. Levchenko and others]. – Sumy "Ukrainian Academy of banking of the NBU". – 46 p.

Dyakonova I. (2008) Methodological foundation for the modernization of the banking supervision in Ukraine on the basis of leading indicators. – Sumy, Ukrainian Academy Of Banking.

EU-Ukraine Association Agreement "Guide to the Association Agreement" (European Commission) – Access mode: http://eeas.europa.eu/archives/docs/images/top_stories/140912_eu-ukraine-associatin-agreement-quick_guide.pdf.

Golovina Y. S. (2015) Crisis regulation of Ukrainian banking system in the period 2014–the first half of 2015: Global and national problems of the economy – V. 7 – Access mode: http://global-national.in.ua/archive/7-2015/141.pdf.

Konopatska L. V. (2008) Banking Supervision: textbook – KNEU. – 336 p.

Kostenko V. V. Retrospective of the formation and development of banking supervision in Ukraine. Economics and state. – 2014. – # 10. – C. 80–84.

Kovalenko M. M. (2011) Government regulation of the banking sector: the essence and components of the mechanism – Access mode: http://www.dridu.dp.ua/vidavnictvo/2011/2011_02(9)/11kmmseu.pdf.

Kovalenko V. V. (2007) International experience in the sphere of prevention and counteraction to laundering of income obtained by criminal means and financing of terrorism: a monograph / V. V. Kovalenko, S. O. Dmitrov, A. V. Yezhov. – Суми: The Ukrainian Academy of banking of the NBU – 112 p.

Kovalenko V. V. (2013) Banking regulation and supervision: methodology and practice: monograph. – 491 p.

Kurdydyk O. (2016) (Pshenychniuk D., Sverdlov I.) Ukrainian financial restructuring: new consensual work-outs for distressed business came into force on 19 October 2016 / DLA Piper. Access mode: https://www.dlapiper.com/en/ukraine/insights/publications/2016/10/ukrainian-financial-restructuring/.

Lepinsky I. (2008) Essence and main characteristics of banking regulation: herald NBU.– #10. – C.66–67.

Leshchenko V. V. (2013) Organizational and legal mechanism of functioning of banking control in Ukraine. – Access mode: http://nbuv.gov.ua/UJRN/Nvamu_upravl_2013_3_36.

Methodological guidelines for the inspection of commercial banks and banking institutions in Ukraine (*Методичні вказівки з інспектування комерційних банків та банківських установ в Україні*): Resolution of the NBU from 30.12.96 # 344 – Access mode: http://zakon.nau.ua.

Methodological instructions for the inspection of banks "Risk Assessment System" (*Методичні вказівки з інспектування банків "Система оцінки ризиків"*): NBU Guidelines from 15.03.2004 # 104 598. – Access mode: http://zakono.rada.gov.ua/laws/show/v0104500-04.

Mishchenko V. I. (2007) Banking operations: Textbook – Kyiv. – Pp. 177 – 205.

Moroz A. M. (2005) The Central Bank and monetary policy: Textbook – Kyiv: KNEU. – 556 p.

National Bank of Ukraine. (2015, May 15). The National Bank of Ukraine announces introduction of new bank capital requirements as well as specific requirements to systemically important banks: https://bank.gov.ua/control/en/publish/printable_article;jsessionid=F29ECD19093B1A289F989E39627405C1?art_id=17537282&showTitle=true.

National Bank of Ukraine. (2016, July 14). Financial sector reform: https://bank.gov.ua/control/en/publish/article?art_id=33820082&cat_id=33820081.

National Bank of Ukraine. (2016, June 4). The National Bank of Ukraine changed the approach to credit risk assessment by banks: https://bank.gov.ua/control/en/publish/printable_article;jsessionid=7C60BD4F398A5D199796155DE4525CED?art_id=32898626&showTitle=true.

National Bank of Ukraine. (2016). Financial draft laws – Access mode: https://bank.gov.ua/control/en/publish/article?art_id=33868732&cat_id=33868731.

National Bank of Ukraine. (2016). Financial stability Report. National Bank of Ukraine – Access mode: https://bank.gov.ua/control/en/publish/category?cat_id=62840775.

National Bank of Ukraine. Comprehensive Program of Ukrainian Financial Sector Development Until 2020 (*Комплексна програма розвитку фінансового сектору України до 2020 р.*) – Access mode: https://bank.gov.ua/control/en/publish/article?art_id=33820088&cat_id=33820087.

NBU internal transformation / National Bank of Ukraine – Access mode: https://bank.gov.ua/control/en/publish/article?art_id=24761917&cat_id=24761916.

Official website of the Deposit Guarantee Fund. – Access mode: http://www.fg.gov.ua/.

On amendments to some Laws Regarding Peculiarities for Financial Recovery Measures for Banks (*Про внесення змін до деяких законодавчих актів України щодо особливостей проведення заходів з фінансового оздоровлення банків*): Law of Ukraine from 24.07.2009 # 1617-VI – Access mode: http://zakon3.rada.gov.ua/laws/show/ru/1617-17.

On amendments to some legislative acts concerning the arrest of assets linked to the financing of terrorism and related financial transactions, stopped in accordance with the decision taken under resolutions of UN Security Council and determine the order of access to such assets (*Про внесення змін до деяких законодавчих актів щодо арешту активів, що пов'язані з фінансуванням тероризму та стосуються фінансових операцій, зупинених до рішення, прийнятого на підставі резолюцій Ради Безпеки ООН, та визначення порядку доступу до таких активів*): Law of Ukraine from 21.04.2011 # 3266-VI – Access mode: http://zakon3.rada.gov.ua/laws/show/3266-17.

On amendments to some legislative acts of the National Bank of Ukraine (*Про внесення змін до деяких нормативно-правових актів Національного банку України*): Resolution of the NBU from 07.06.2016 # 341. – Access mode: http://zakon4.rada.gov.ua/laws/show/v0341500-16.

On amendments to some Legislative Acts of Ukraine regarding liability associated with the bank individuals (*Про внесення змін до деяких законодавчих актів України щодо відповідальності пов'язаних із банком осіб*): Law of Ukraine # 218-VIII from 02.03.2015. – Access mode: http://zakon4.rada.gov.ua/laws/show/218-19.

On amendments to the Resolution of the Board of the National Bank of Ukraine (*Про внесення змін до постанови Правління Національного банку України від 18 грудня 2014 року № 820*) from 18.12.2014 # 820: Resolution of the NBU from 17.03.2016 # 170 – Access mode: http://zakon3.rada.gov.ua/laws/show/v0170500-16/paran2#n2.

On approval of Instruction of regulation of Bank Activities in Ukraine (*Про затвердження Інструкції про порядок регулювання діяльності банків в Україні*): Resolution of the NBU from 28.08.2001 # 368 – Access mode: http://zakon5.rada.gov.ua/laws/show/z0841-01/page 5.

On approval of methodological recommendations on the development of banks of Ukraine programs with the aim of combating the legalization (laundering) of money obtained by criminal means (*Про схвалення Методичних рекомендацій з питань розроблення банками України програм з метою протидії легалізації (відмиванню) грошей, отриманих злочинним шляхом*): Resolution of the NBU from 30.04.02 # 164. – Access mode: http://zakon3.rada.gov.ua/laws/show/v0164500-02.

On Approval of Methodological Recommendations on the Organization and Functioning of Risk Management Systems in Banks of Ukraine (*Про схвалення Методичних рекомендацій щодо організації та функціонування систем ризик-менеджменту в банках України*): Resolution of the NBU from 02.08.2004 # 361 – Access mode: http://zakon4.rada.gov.ua/laws/show/v0361500-04.

On approval of requirements on organization of financial monitoring by entities of initial financial monitoring (*Про затвердження Вимог до організації фінансового моніторингу суб'єктами первинного фінансового у сфері запобігання та протидії запровадженню в легальний обіг доходів, одержаних злочинним шляхом, та фінансуванню тероризму*): The order of the State Department of financial monitoring from 24.04.2003 # 40. – Access mode: http://zakon5.rada.gov.ua/laws/show/z0337-03.

On approval of the definition of banks in Ukraine credit risk from active banking operations (*Про затвердження Положення про визначення банками України розміру кредитного ризику за активними банківськими операціями*): Resolution of the NBU from 30.06.2016 # 351 – Access mode: http://zakon3.rada.gov.ua/laws/show/v0351500-16/page.

On approval of the foundations of the interest rate policy of the National bank of Ukraine (*Про затвердження Положення про основи процентної політики Національного банку України*): Resolution of the NBU from 21.04.2016 # 277 – Access mode: http://zakon3.rada.gov.ua/laws/show/v0277500-16.

On Approval of the Instruction on the Procedure for Regulating and Analyzing the Activities of Commercial Banks (*Про затвердження Інструкції про порядок регулювання аналіз діяльності комерційних банків*): Resolution of the NBU from 14.04.1998 # 141 – Access mode: http://zakon2.rada.gov.ua/laws/show/z0323-98.

On Approval of the Methodology for Calculation of Economic Norms for Regulating the Activities of Banks in Ukraine (*Про схвалення Методики розрахунку економічних нормативів регулювання діяльності банків в Україні*): Resolution of the NBU from 02.06.2009 # 315 – Access mode: http://zakono.rada.gov.ua/laws/show/v0315500-09.

On approval of the procedure for granting banks and branches of foreign banks general licenses for currency transactions (*Про затвердження деяких нормативно-правових актів Національного банку України*): Act of NBU from 08.09.2011 # 306 – Access mode: http://zakono.rada.gov.ua/laws/show/z1203-11.

On approval of the procedure of deposit transactions of Ukrainian banks with corporations and individuals (*Про затвердження Положення про порядок здійснення банками України вкладних (депозитних) операцій з юридичними і фізичними особами*): Resolution of the NBU from 3.02.2003 # 516 – Access mode: http://zakon5.rada.gov.ua/laws/show/z1256-03.

On approval of the Regulation of economic standards for the actions of commercial banks (*Про затвердження Положення про економічні нормативи регулювання діяльності комерційних банків*): Resolution of the NBU from 21.12.1993 # 114. – Access mode: http://zakon2.rada.gov.ua/laws/show/v0114500-93.

On approval of the regulation on the implementation by banks of financial monitoring (*Про затвердження Положення про здійснення банками фінансового моніторингу*): Resolution of the NBU from 14.05.03 # 189. – Access mode: http://zakon5.rada.gov.ua/laws/show/z0381-03.

On approval of the Regulation on the Procedure for Organizing and Conducting Inspections on Prevention and Counteraction to the Legalization (Laundering) of the Proceeds from Crime or the Financing of Terrorism (*Про затвердження Положення про порядок організації та проведення перевірок з питань запобігання та протидії легалізації (відмиванню) доходів, одержаних злочинним шляхом, фінансуванню тероризму та фінансуванню розповсюдження зброї масового знищення*): Resolution of the NBU from 20.06.2011 # 197 – Access mode: http://zakon5.rada.gov.ua/laws/show/z0852-11.

On approving plan of activities for 2015 of prevention and counteraction to legalization (laundering) of income from crime, terrorist financing and financing of proliferation of weapons of mass destruction (*Про затвердження плану заходів на 2015 рік із запобігання та протидії легалізації (відмиванню) доходів, одержаних злочинним шляхом, фінансуванню тероризму та фінансуванню розповсюдження зброї масового знищення*): Resolution of the Cabinet of Ministers of Ukraine and the National Bank of Ukraine from 11.03.2015 # 99. – Access mode: http://zakon3.rada.gov.ua/laws/show/99-2015-П.

On banks and banking activity (*Про банки і банківську діяльність*): Law of Ukraine from 18.01.2018 # 2121–14 – Access mode: http://zakon3.rada.gov.ua/laws/show/2121-14.

On financial services and state regulation of financial markets (*Про фінансові послуги та державне регулювання ринків фінансових послуг*): Law of Ukraine from 12.07.2001 # 2664-III – Access mode: http://zakon3.rada.gov.ua/laws/show/2664-14.

On Financial Services and State Regulation of Financial Services Markets (*Про фінансові послуги та державне регулювання ринків фінансових послуг*): Law of Ukraine from 12.07.2001 # 2664-III. – Access mode: http://zakon3.rada.gov.ua/laws/show/2664-14.

On Forty recommendations of the Group from development of financial measures of fight against money laundering (FATF) (*Про Сорок рекомендацій Групи з розробки фінансових заходів боротьби з відмиванням грошей (FATF)*): Joint resolution of the Cabinet of Ministers of Ukraine and the National Bank of Ukraine from 28.08.01 # 1124. – Access mode: http://zakon5.rada.gov.ua/laws/show/1124-2001-%D0%BF.

On Households Deposit Guarantee System (*Про систему гарантування вкладів фізичних осіб*): Law of Ukraine from 23.02.2012 # 4452-VI – Access mode http://zakon4.rada.gov.ua/laws/show/4452-17.

On increase of capital of Ukrainian banks (*Про збільшення капіталу банків України*): Resolution of the NBU from 04.02.2016 # 58 – Access mode: http://zakon2.rada.gov.ua/laws/show/v0058500-16.

On measures aimed at enhancing capitalization and restructuring of banks (*Про заходи, спрямовані на сприяння капіталізації та реструктуризації банків*): Resolution of the VRU from 28.12.2014 # 78-VIII – Access mode: http://zakon0.rada.gov.ua/laws/show/78-19-VI.

On prevention and counteraction to legalization (laundering) of income obtained by criminal means (*Про запобігання та протидію легалізації (відмиванню) доходів, одержаних злочинним шляхом, або фінансуванню тероризму*): Law of Ukraine from 28.11.02 N° 249-IV. – Access mode: http://zakon5.rada.gov.ua/laws/show/249-15.

On prevention and counteraction to legalization (laundering) of income from crime, terrorist financing and financing of proliferation of weapons of mass destruction (*Про запобігання та протидію легалізації (відмиванню) доходів, одержаних злочинним шляхом, фінансуванню тероризму та фінансуванню розповсюдження зброї масового знищення*): Law of Ukraine from 14.10.2014 # 1702-VII – Access mode: http://zakon5.rada.gov.ua/laws/show/1702-18.

On resolving the situation in the money and foreign exchange markets of Ukraine (*Про врегулювання ситуації на грошово-кредитному та валютному ринках України*): Resolution of the NBU from 07.06.2016 # 342. – Access mode: http://zakon3.rada.gov.ua/laws/show/v0342500-16.

On the application by the National Bank of Ukraine of the measures of influence for violation of banking laws (*Про затвердження Положення про застосування Національним банком України заходів впливу за порушення банківського законодавства*): Resolution of the NBU from 28.08.2001 # 369 – Access mode: http://zakon5.rada.gov.ua/laws/show/z0845-01.

On the application of the National bank of Ukraine measures of impact (*Про затвердження Положення про застосування Національним банком України заходів впливу*): Resolution of the NBU from 17.08.2012 # 346 – Access mode: http://zakon3.rada.gov.ua/laws/show/z1590-12.

On the application of the National bank of Ukraine standard instruments regulating banking system liquidity (*Про затвердження Положення про застосування Національним банком України стандартних інструментів регулювання ліквідності банківської системи*): Resolution of the NBU from 17.09.2015 # 615 – Access mode: http://zakon5.rada.gov.ua/laws/show/v0615500-15.

On the approval of the resolution on definition of bank related persons from 12.05.2015 # 315 (*Про затвердження Положення про визначення пов'язаних із банком осіб*): Resolution of the National Bank of Ukraine – Access mode: http://zakon3.rada.gov.ua/laws/show/v0315500-15.

On the change of order of forming and storage of mandatory reserves (*Про зміну порядку формування та зберігання обов'язкових резервів*): Resolution of the NBU from 18.12.2014 # 820 – Access mode: http://zakon3.rada.gov.ua/laws/show/v0820500-14.

On the Commission of the National Bank of Ukraine on Supervision and Regulation of Banks (*Про Положення про Комісію Національного банку України питань нагляду та регулювання діяльності банків*): Resolution of the NBU from 09.11.98 # 470. – Access mode: http://zakon2.rada.gov.ua/laws/show/v0470500-98.

On The Deposit Guarantee Fund for Individuals Deposits (*Про Фонд гарантування вкладів фізичних осіб*): Law of Ukraine from 20.09.2001 # 2740-III. – Access mode: http:// http://zakon3.rada.gov.ua/laws/show/2740-14.

On the Guaranteeing of Deposits of Individuals (*Про систему гарантування вкладів фізичних осіб*): Resolution of the NBU from 23.02.2012 # 4452-VI – Access mode: http://zakon4.rada.gov.ua/laws/show/4452-17.

On the method for calculating economic standards of regulation of banks in Ukraine (*Про схвалення Методики розрахунку економічних нормативів регулювання діяльності банків в Україні*): Resolution of the NBU from 02.06.2009 # 315 – Access mode: http://zakon2.rada.gov.ua/laws/show/v0315500-09.

On the National Bank of Ukraine (*Про Національний банк України*): Law of Ukraine from 20.05.1999 # 679-XIV – Access mode: http://zakon2.rada.gov.ua/laws/show/679-14.

On the National Bank of Ukraine: Law of Ukraine from 20.05.1999 # 679-XIV. – Access mode: http://zakon4.rada.gov.ua/laws/show/679-14.

On the order of regulation of banks' activity in Ukraine (*Про затвердження Інструкції про порядок регулювання діяльності банків в Україні*): Resolution of the NBU from 28.08.2001 # 368 – Access mode: http://zakon2.rada.gov.ua/laws/show/z0841-01.

On the planning and conducting of inspections (*Про затвердження Положення про організацію та проведення інспекційних перевірок*): Resolution of the NBU from 17.07.2001 # 276 – Access mode: http://zakon2.rada.gov.ua/laws/show/z0703-01.

On the procedure for banks registration and licensing, opening of stand-alone offices (*Про порядок реєстрації та ліцензування банків, відкриття відокремлених підрозділів*): Resolution of the NBU from 08.09.2011 # 306 – Access mode: http://zakon2.rada.gov.ua/laws/show/z1203-11.

On the procedure for compiling and publishing financial statements of banks of Ukraine (*Про затвердження Інструкції порядок складання та оприлюднення фінансової звітності банків України*): Resolution of the NBU from 07.12.2004 # 598. – Access mode: http://zakon2.rada.gov.ua/laws/show/z1660-04.

On the procedure for determination of ratings on rating system CAMELS (*Про затвердження Інструкції порядок складання та оприлюднення звітності банків України*): Resolution of the NBU from 08.05.2002 # 171 – Access mode: http://zakon2.rada.gov.ua/laws/show/v0171500-02.

On the Procedure for Granting Banking Licenses for Banking Operations (*Про затвердження Положення про порядок видачі банкам ліцензії на здійснення банківських операцій*): Resolution of the NBU from 06.05.98 # 181 – Access mode: http://zakon3.rada.gov.ua/laws/show/z0373-98.

On the Procedure for Regulating the Activities of Banks in Ukraine (*Про затвердження Інструкції про порядок регулювання діяльності банків в Україні*): Resolution of the NBU from 28.08.2001 # 368. – Access mode: http://zakon3.rada.gov.ua/laws/show/z0841-01.

On the procedure for the creation, registration of commercial banks (*Тимчасове положення про порядок створення, реєстрації комерційних банків і здійснення нагляду за їх діяльністю*): Temporary provision of the NBU from 17.07.92 # 16. – Access mode: http://zakon2.rada.gov.ua/laws/show/v0016500-92.

On the Procedure for the Establishment and Registration of Commercial Banks and On the Procedure for Licensing Banks in Ukraine (*Про затвердження положень "Про порядок створення і реєстрації комерційних банків" та "Про порядок банків в Україні"*): Resolution of the NBU from 27.03.96 # 77. – Access mode: http://zakon3.rada.gov.ua/laws/show/v0077500-96.

On the procedure of cash operations in the national economy of Ukraine (*Порядок ведення касових операцій у національній валюті в Україні*): Resolution of the Board of the National Bank of Ukraine from 02.02.1995 # 228. – Access mode: http://zakon3.rada.gov.ua/laws/show/v0228500-95.

On the procedure of formation of reserves on loans and accrued interests on them and bad debts writing-off for banks (*Про затвердження Порядку формування банками резервів за кредитами і нарахованими за ними процентами та списання безнадійної заборгованості*): Resolution of the NBU from 13.09.2010 # 424 – Access mode: http://zakon2.rada.gov.ua/laws/show/z0998-10.

On the procedure of issuing to banks of banking licenses, written permits and licenses to perform certain operations (*Про затвердження Положення про порядок видачі банківських ліцензій, письмових дозволів та ліцензій на виконання окремих операцій*): Resolution of the NBU from 17.07.2001 # 275 – Access mode: http://zakon2.rada.gov.ua/laws/show/z0730-01.

On the structure of the system of banking supervision of the National Bank of Ukraine and its authority to adequately respond to violations in the activities of commercial banks (*Про затвердження Положення "Про структуру системи банківського нагляду Національного банку України його повноваження щодо адекватного реагування на порушення в діяльності комерційних банків"*): Resolution of the NBU from 17.11.97 # 380. – Access mode: http://zakon2.rada.gov.ua/laws/show/v0486500-97.

On the System of Currency Regulation and Currency Control (*Про систему валютного регулювання і валютного контролю*): Decree of the Cabinet of The Ministers of Ukraine from 25.11.1993 # 3651-XII. – Access mode: http://zakon3.rada.gov.ua/laws/show/15-93.

On the System of Risk Assessment: Resolution of the NBU from 15.03.2004 # 104 – Access mode: http://zakon2.rada.gov.ua/laws/show/v0104500-04.

On the Unified state information system in the sphere of prevention and counteraction to legalization (laundering) of income obtained by criminal means and financing of terrorism (*Про Єдину державну інформаційну систему сфері запобігання та протидії легалізації (відмиванню) доходів, одержаних злочинним шляхом, і фінансуванню тероризму*): Resolution of the Cabinet of Ministers of Ukraine from 10.12.2003 # 1896. – Access mode: http://zakon3.rada.gov.ua/laws/show/1896-2003-%D0%BF?test=GqsMfB7.apXV2m7EZiDeaueiHI46Ys80msh8Ie6.

Rajewski K. E. (2003) Banking Supervision: Educational-methodical manual for self-learning. – Kyiv. – 174 p.

Some issues of the Unified state information system in the sphere of prevention and counteraction to legalization (laundering) of income from crime, terrorist financing and financing of proliferation of weapons of mass destruction (*Деякі питання Єдиної державної інформаційної системи у сфері запобігання та протидії легалізації (відмиванню) доходів, одержаних злочинним шляхом, фінансуванню тероризму та фінансуванню розповсюдження зброї масового знищення*): Resolution of the Cabinet of Ministers of Ukraine from 14.05.2015 # 299. – Access mode: http://zakon3.rada.gov.ua/laws/show/299-2015-П.

The National Bank of Ukraine continues to temper currency regulation: NBU on 08.06.2016 – Access mode: http://www.bank.gov.ua/control/uk/publish/article?art_id=32236335.

Ukraine: law on consumer lending adopted (2016) / CMS Law-Now. Access mode: http://www.cms-lawnow.com/ealerts/2016/11/ukraine-law-on-consumer-lending-adopted.

www.ingramcontent.com/pod-product-compliance
Lightning Source LLC
Chambersburg PA
CBHW031332230926
51848CB00001B/199
*9789004381414*